DEALING WITH
TRAUMA

AN INTRODUCTORY GUIDE TO SHARPEN
YOUR PRACTICAL COUNSELLING SKILLS

DR JIMMY HENDERSON

ISBN 978-0-620-86749-8 (Print Edition)

ISBN 978-0-620-86750-4 (eBook Edition)

Cover and interior crafted with love by www.myebook.online

MYEBOOK
WE EMPOWER AUTHORS

IMPORTANT

This training has been split into two parts.

In part one I briefly introduce trauma and explain some important differences between 'debriefing' and 'trauma counselling', show what conditions are necessary for a good counselling environment, present a simple, five-stage counselling approach which I have previously used with success, a number of important trauma counselling skills, as well as practical assessments and role plays for training lay-counsellors. Throughout the guide I also use a number of short case studies to show you how to use the skills correctly and also give other useful tips.

I will be using the term 'clients' in these guides as it is more appropriate than 'traumatised people' and identifies them as the persons whom you are busy counselling. I will also use the word 'story' to denote their sharing the details of the incident. This is not meant to downplay their experience as only a 'story', but rather it is an attempt to organise their account of the incident into a coherent whole.

In part two I have placed a number of full-length case studies which are practical examples of how to do trauma counselling in real-life settings. It is a good idea to have both of these guides on hand when doing counselling.

I hope that you will find these guides useful for your own counselling or when training new lay-counsellors.

Best wishes ·

Jimmy Henderson

DISCLAIMER

I have not shown references to every section in this book as it is not a trauma textbook. It is only a guide to trauma counselling for lay counsellors or care-givers.

Although I have made every effort to make sure it is accurate and relevant, I cannot be sure that it is 100% up to date or that I have not left out some sections that should have been included.

ACKNOWLEDGEMENTS

This guide has been a long time in the making and I needed the support of a number of people.

It has been a long and difficult road and I am grateful for all this help I received. I especially wish to thank my editor and publisher David Henderson of www.myebook.online for his encouragement, support, editing, publishing and marketing of this guide.

For those of you who also wish to self-publish, I recommend www.myebook.online the company that handled my e-book conversion and placed it on Amazon for your benefit.

INTRODUCTION

Welcome to the world of trauma counselling. This guide has been specially prepared for those of you involved in care-giving, church or lay-counselling or the training of lay (volunteer) counsellors. But actually, it will also be useful for anyone to improve their present counselling skills when dealing with the real distress that comes with trauma.

I have written this guide in such a way as to give you, as care-givers, lay counsellors or volunteers working in the community, the basic skills and understanding of trauma to help you develop an empathetic ear and a caring approach to dealing with people who have been exposed to trauma

I must point out again that this guide is not referenced as it is not meant as a textbook for professional therapists. You need to remember that lay-counsellors are actually not qualified to deal with trauma and you should refer anyone with serious symptoms to qualified and registered professionals. However, it can happen that, in an emergency, you could be called upon to help people that have been traumatised by a serious event in their lives, or by some sort of disaster. And in this case, you must do what you can.

Finally, we do sometimes get traumatised persons phoning in for help. I must point out that telephone or online counselling is really not a good idea for people who have been recently and seriously traumatised, as they will really need plenty of hands-on support. If the trauma is in the distant past it may be possible to help them over the phone.

CONTENTS

PART ONE

Training for lay counsellors

CHAPTER ONE

EXPLAINING TRAUMA

THE DIFFERENCE BETWEEN A CRISIS AND TRAUMA

I notice how many people confuse trauma when they say how they were traumatised by this or that happening, when it is not trauma as such, but rather a **crisis**. There are important differences between a crisis and real trauma, and it is important that you know them so that you will be able to recognise and respond properly.

Most of us face challenges on a daily basis, but they are usually temporary and can be dealt with quite quickly. For instance, a car accident, a shortage of cash, not having a place to stay after a break-up, the loss of a pet, a bad relationship with a family member and a split-up with a spouse or partner.

Some of these situations can even be devastating, especially those in which a person is exposed to it for a long time, such as emotional abuse, a divorce, being retrenched and becoming destitute, the death of a loved one, being a victim of crime and the insidious pain of loneliness, especially for the elderly and abandoned. I am sure that many of us have gone through a similar experience and have sought help or counselling of some sort. To the person experiencing it, these events are painful and overwhelming at the time, but somehow we get through them and life goes on. These are what we call 'crises', events which are common to most people, relatively short-lived and can be resolved over in time with a bit of help. This is not trauma.

Trauma is a worst-case scenario, and involves serious incidents all having something in common, that the person is confronted with death or the threat of death or serious injury to themselves, their loved ones or their friends. Death or the fear of death are the key words here, and this type of event is usually unexpected, random and not commonplace at all.

Some typical examples of traumatic events would be natural or man-made disasters, being victims of violent crime (very prevalent in this country at this time), hijackings, robberies, rape or serious assaults, being caught up in public violence, or involved in a very serious motor-vehicle accident. In fact, trauma can occur even when one is only a witness to seriously violent situations such as war or rioting. These are the times when one feels totally helpless and out-of-control. Trauma can also be worsened by other factors, such as grieving over the death of a spouse or loved one which resulted from the same violent incident.

These situations all result in powerful emotions such as fear, horror and helplessness, as well as a complete loss of control, and these need immediate attention. In trauma counselling it is also very important to deal with any negative thoughts or groundless beliefs about what clients feel that they could have, or should have done during the incident, as these only feed their crippling emotions.

Trauma is also very visual and those affected will often complain of vivid images of the scene, the perpetrators, the weapons, or dead bodies disturbing their every waking moment. If we add to this unpleasant package the memory of smells, sounds or verbal threats from the incident, the terrible effects of trauma can clearly be seen.

THE DIFFERENCES BETWEEN TRAU-MA COUNSELLING AND TRAUMA DE-BRIEFING

Trauma counselling is not the same as 'debriefing'. Trauma *debriefing*, as the name suggests, is a brief group-counselling session which is usually used as a first line of counselling when a number of people have experienced or been caught up in the same traumatic incident, such as a natural or man-made disaster, an armed robbery at their place of work or when shopping or banking. In fact, seeing or even hearing about a violent incident or accident, especially involving family or friends, can lead to trauma.

DEBRIEFING A GROUP OF PEOPLE

When debriefing, those affected by the incident should be asked to sit together in a group and, depending on the amount of people in the group (which should not be more than eight, a manageable amount for one counsellor) and the time available, be allowed to briefly share their experiences, feelings and thoughts about what happened. During this time they will each get a brief period of counselling from the counsellor, and hopefully also the support and encouragement of the rest of the group.

Details of the whole process from beginning to end can be found in the group debriefing scenario in part two of the guide.

Although debriefing gives the opportunity for group-counselling, it is not as effective as one-on-one counselling which is more structured and comprehensive, as the main purpose of debriefing is to offer quick support to a number of people to lessen the early impact of trauma.

You may find that some persons in the group may not have been directly exposed to the incident and need less trauma counselling or even none at all. Debriefing is therefore also useful as a first step in seeing which persons in the group need individual trauma counselling. You can decide this after observing their behaviour and body-language. More traumatised members of the group will be less in control of their emotions and their body language will be very defensive. These persons must be asked to stay for in-depth trauma counselling after the debriefing.

THE DIFFERENT PHASES OF TRAUMA

Trauma unfolds over three different phases, and each can be identified by a number of symptoms. What actually happens is that those people who have been traumatised have a sudden and very powerful stress response to the specific incident, which, even with the proper treatment, can take as long as eight weeks to lessen and return to normal. If their stress is not managed effectively, they can develop Post-Traumatic Stress Disorder (P.T.S.D), a very serious condition which needs intensive treatment.

The three different phases unfold over a period of weeks, and each has its own set of symptoms. It is important to know which phase which your client is in when counselling, as you will need to use different approaches and skills for each phase.

The three phases are:

The 'impact' or acute phase

The 'recoil' phase

And finally, after a time of healing, a 're-organisation and re-integration' phase

Let me explain each of these phases. Try to notice the differences.

PHASE 1: THE IMPACT OR ACUTE PHASE

This is the first phase and usually happens immediately after the incident on the same day (within an hour). However, in some cases the symptoms can be delayed by up to a week.

Identifying this phase

Looking at your clients' behaviour

Some of them may seem frozen, numbed, or shocked by what has happened, and could even return to early childhood behaviours such as curling up in the foetal position when they lie down. This happens because of their protective coping mechanisms which have now kicked in. Their actions during this phase will most likely reveal shock, disbelief and a loss of contact with reality. They could also be slow to respond to your questions, and will usually be quite helpless, disorientated and confused and not able to make sense. On the other hand, people do have different *coping styles* when they are traumatised, and some of your clients in this first phase could do just the opposite, such as being very agitated and upset, even hysterical and out-of-control.

Noting your clients' emotions

During first phase of trauma their most common emotions will be fear, terror and horror. These are the result of their having had such a terrible personal experience, or else witnessing something which has caused the trauma, such as seeing the body of a dead relative or the mangled victims of some natural disaster.

Looking at their symptoms

Persons who have been traumatised and are in the impact or acute phase, may have all or at least some of the following symptoms: headaches, nausea, vomiting, stomach pains and diarrhoea. Any medical issues they have will also get worse. At night they could have problems sleeping and also have nightmares. In the days that follow they will usually not be able to concentrate on work or any household tasks and may also have constant vivid images (flashbacks) together with distress and negative thoughts about the event.

Counselling during this phase

Try to begin counselling within an hour of the incident, as trauma-tised persons may try to cope by creating what is called a '*traumatic envelope*', a state of mind in which they are less likely or willing to talk or share details of the traumatic incident with anyone, even a counsellor.

If the incident has just taken place, give more practical support. Comfort them with compassion and empathy. Remember that the scene of a tragic accident or violent traumatic incident is usually chaotic, with police and emergency services attending to injured victims and traumatised persons. You will not be able to do proper trauma counselling under these conditions. Medical treatment is a priority in such cases, and you may only be able to counsel them once they have been taken to hospital, properly treated, are conscious and able to speak.

Provide structure, support and guidance to your clients during this first phase, as they will need help with transport and in completing any official statements. Also ask their families and friends for help with these tasks to spread the load wherever possible.

As soon as it is practical, begin with 'light 'counselling. Just be *fully* present and help them express any feelings and thoughts which emerge spontaneously without passing judgement. As soon as it is possible, move them to a suitable room or area for proper counselling. If they wish for some of their family or friends to be present for additional support, that is fine. This is also a good idea if you are a male counsellor and are counselling a female client who has been sexually assaulted. She will feel more comfortable speaking to you with another female friend or relative there for support.

While you are doing this you can also try getting them to do some deep breathing and relaxation techniques to help them relax. These are discussed under the section of empowerment skills.

As you will see later, it is important to build a good relationship of trust with your clients early on. Begin by reassuring them that you are there to help, give support and *normalise* their symptoms. This means explaining to them that their feelings of fear, confusion, helplessness and loss of control, as well as any nausea, stomach pains and heart palpitations, are not cause for concern, as they are typical and normal under the circumstances. This will re-assure them.

PHASE 2: THE RECOIL PHASE

This phase starts within a few hours after the incident, once the traumatised person's coping mechanisms have kicked in, and can carry on for a few weeks.

Identifying this phase

Looking at your client's behaviour

During this phase your clients may be less co-operative and may simply wish to be left alone. This means that the 'traumatic envelope' we spoke about earlier has come into play as a result of their out-of-control emotions and the severe stress they are going through. This highlights why it is so important to support them within an hour to build an early relationship of trust which will hopefully prevent this happening.

Noting their emotions

This recoil phase can last for several weeks, during which time your clients will most likely be highly anxious, very fearful and also feel helpless and insecure. However, they may also become angry or irritable for no real reason at all, and you will have to be careful not to upset them by saying the wrong thing.

Another reason for their irritability is that they may also be feeling guilty for something they did (or did not do), leading up to, or during the incident, and are judging or blaming themselves. Trauma survivors often feel that there was more that they could have done to either prevent or change the outcome of the situation. If you question them you might find that they are often sad, apathetic and depressed. However, at other times they can be overcome with emotion, feel totally out of control and believe that everything is too much to bear. Experiencing trauma puts people on an emotional rollercoaster and it is important to explain to your clients that this is perfectly normal.

Identifying negative images and thoughts

During counselling, apart from the emotions already mentioned, your clients may also complain of worrying images of the incident (called 'flashbacks') which pop up spontaneously. This is most likely to happen if they see something that reminds them of the incident (cues), such as someone who resembles their attacker, or the anniversary of the death of a loved one killed in the incident. This can have the effect that they are continually re-living the trauma. Identify these images for in-depth exploring, as they are very important.

Thoughts become self-talk

In trauma you will find that your clients' emotions, thoughts and actions are interwoven, and that the powerful emotions are kept going by negative thoughts, misguided perceptions and irrational beliefs linked to the incident. These thoughts enter their minds as *internal conversations or self-talk* which they will mull over time and time again, and have a powerful effect on how they behave.

For example,

'I could have done more'

'I caused this'

'I am a failure'

'I am a coward'

This ongoing self-talk becomes more and more negative and will have to be addressed quickly.

Observing their symptoms

The symptoms that will most likely be reported by your clients in this (second) phase will be feeling ill, being unable to concentrate and sleep, and if they do sleep, being plagued by nightmares. They might also be forgetful and feel sometimes detached from reality. During this time they might show very little interest in going out or getting involved in other social activities.

Counselling this phase

Counselling is very important during this phase. Encourage your clients to begin to share their story and their feelings of pain, fear and horror more deeply. However, be careful not to let them fully re-live the incident or they could be *re-traumatised*. If they are very distressed, rather keep them at an *emotional distance* from the incident. This will be explained later.

During this phase, encourage your clients to get practical day-to-day help and support from their families and friends to share the load with household tasks such as cooking, transporting children and other responsibilities and also encourage some sort of routine to give them a feeling of control over their lives. The sense of being in control is usually lost during a traumatic incident, and it is important that you help your clients restore this as soon as possible.

PHASE 3: THE RE-ORGANISATION AND RE-IN-TEGRATION PHASE

This is the last phase of the trauma process by which time you should see your clients' lives slowly returning to normal and they would be showing less stress. If your counselling sessions have been successful this will take about one to two months.

Identifying the final phase

Seeing improvement in your clients' symptoms

After a few months of counselling, your clients will begin to cope much better and start managing their normal household routines without help. Their emotions will be more under control and any problems with sleeping or eating should have largely disappeared. Their thinking will also become more positive and they should have returned to their earlier social lives and activities. Any medical problems should also have improved by stage three.

If their symptoms have not improved after this time, refer them to a psychologist or psychiatrist, as they could be developing post-traumatic stress disorder (P.T.S.D). You, as lay counsellors or care-givers, are not qualified (or allowed by law) to treat P.T.S.D, which I will briefly discuss in the next section. If their trauma is not dealt with or resolved after three months, they could also end up with other problems such as depression or eating disorders. Rather be safe than sorry.

Counselling this final phase

This is when you help your clients find some closure and integrate the experience into their lives. Empower them by helping them restore their shattered self-esteem, regain their feeling of control and let go of any leftover feelings of self-blame and guilt. This phase includes the final stage of mastery in which you guide your clients towards finding meaning and purpose in their lives and to develop plans for their future.

HAVING MORE THAN ONE COUNSELLING SESSION

It is highly unlikely that you will be able to do proper trauma counselling in only one session unless your clients have received help earlier and have moved into final phase of healing. It is best that your counselling be spread out over a number of sessions in a time of about eight (8) weeks, as the symptoms and phases unfold in different ways during this time.

I also advise you not to try to counsel persons in the *impact or acute phase* (immediately following the incident) using online portals or over the phone, as they will be very distressed and will need plenty of support and personal face-to-face attention. If this happens, rather arrange for face-to-face counselling as soon as possible, even if it means that you have to go to their homes. Many counselling centres or large companies have call-out counselling teams on standby and this would be the time to use them. Also arrange for them to have more than one session or visits.

In the case where a number of persons have been involved in the traumatic incident, you will need to arrange either with counselling centre staff or, in the case of on-site counselling at businesses or factories, with their manager, for them to be counselled one at a time. Remember that trauma counselling is not the same as trauma debriefing. This will be fully explained later.

Let us briefly look at each session and what approach and skills are needed. If you wish you can study the different skills in more depth at this time by turning to the chapter on counselling skills. (Chapter four). However, I would suggest that you rather wait until you have reached chapter four, as this is just a rough outline of the sessions so that you can get a basic feel for the process at this time.

The first session

Your first session should be within an hour of the incident if is at all possible. This will allow you to help them through the *impact* phase when they are most vulnerable and need immediate support.

Your aim is to build a strong rapport and a good relationship and provide them with this support. These skills, as well as those of listening, reflection and questioning, will be discussed in detail in a later section.

Begin by introducing yourself using your first name, telling them that you are a trauma counsellor and are here to help. Assure them that you will be with them all the way through this process. They must not feel that they are alone in this difficult journey.

Continue building your relationship by normalising their symptoms and emotions and then invite them to share what they are feeling at that moment. Reflect their emotions (name them) and give immediate empathetic responses. You should try to remember each emotion, as later on, you will have to give each of these emotions special attention and use a different approach.

If your clients are very tense and unable to relax, try letting them do deep breathing and relaxation exercises. This may help them. See the section on 'Empowerment skills'.

Sharing their feelings with you should hopefully help them let go of tension by crying or sobbing. This is a good sign. Do not stop them from expressing their pain in this way. Rather encourage them to breathe, feel and acknowledge each emotion coming through. Your job is to reflect and explore these emotions as they emerge. During 'exploring' we ask clients to share the feelings and emotions they felt at every step of the incident (frame by frame).

At the same time, ask your clients to share any self-recriminating thoughts or negative self-beliefs that they have, but do not challenge them on these beliefs at this time, as they are still vulnerable. This will come later during the stage of 'empowerment'. Just remember them for the next session.

Exploring emotions and thoughts should take up most of the first session and hopefully bring your clients some relief which will allow them to manage for a day or two until the next session. This means that in the first session you should not normally go beyond stages two and three of the trauma counselling process as suggested in this guide.

Finally, at the end of the first session, give your clients some practical advice for handling their day-to-day issues and coping with their stress until the next session. For example, they must get medical attention for serious symptoms, watch what they eat and drink due to stomach upsets; try not to block out the stress with pain-killers or alcohol as this will only drag the process of healing on for longer; and, unless they have family at home who are supporting them through the crisis, to rather return to work the next day. However, if they have stressful positions they should rather ask for light duties where they can be supported by work colleagues and brought to the counselling centre for later sessions. The bottom line here is that it is not a good idea to leave a traumatised person alone at home without any form of support as this could lead to over-thinking and more distress and despair.

The second session

Arrange session two for the following day, that is, within twenty-four hours of the incident. Family members or friends should bring your clients to the counselling centre, as it not advisable for them to drive when they are in a bad state of mind.

If you are assisting your clients at their place of work as part of an employee assistance program, you will need to travel to meet and greet them at their entrance, accompany them inside and ask their manager for a private office where you can do your counselling.

Begin by asking your clients how they are feeling and what they are still thinking, as well as if any new symptoms have emerged since the previous day. Reflect this back to them to get clarification. Specifically ask about any negative thoughts and distressing images which they may have experienced during the night. At this time you can encourage your clients to share their feelings and thoughts in more detail while you respond empathetically. Having settled during the night, they may be able to share more than they did in session one when they desperately needed on-hand support and re-assurances.

During this session you should try to finish stage three (exploring negative thoughts and beliefs) and move into stage four, that of *empowerment*. At this time you begin to challenge their negative self-talk and irrational beliefs which you identified during the first session. The idea here is to counter or refute these thoughts and beliefs. However, do not place pressure on your clients with challenging if they are still in distress. Rather stay with their feelings until their emotions improve.

If, by the end of this session, your clients have not responded well, and you have not been able to help them reduce their stress and tension, there may be complicating factors which you are not aware of, and they should be referred to a qualified professional for long-term help.

The third session

Arrange the third session for a few days later, either at the counselling centre or your clients' place of work as before. Your focus during this session should be on *empowerment* (stage four), but you can try to move into stage five (option-handling) if they respond well to stage four. The process of empowerment means challenging your client's thoughts about the incident with objectivity and positive truths in order to help them let go of the distressing feelings associated with these beliefs.

This is discussed fully in the section on counselling skills (empowerment).

As you introduce stage five, help them explore realistic ideas and options which they believe will enable them to cope better in the long term and give them a sense of control over their lives again. This means putting together a *plan for mastery* which may include them having to see doctors, lawyers or other professionals to help them deal with the consequences of the incident.

You can use more of a thinking approach during this session, as most of your clients' emotions and self-recriminating thoughts and beliefs should, by now, have been dealt with. However, if any distress or disturbing thoughts do resurface, offer immediate support, even if this means returning to the earlier stages.

The fourth session

This session can be scheduled for about two weeks later and in this case, you should try to focus on the final stage of the trauma counselling process, that of mastery.

Your clients' earlier out-of-control feelings, such as fear, helplessness, guilt or self-blame, as well as their negative perceptions and self-talk, should hopefully have been properly managed by this time, and they should be in a position to discuss their plan to return normality to their lives. Have a look at their plan and see what they have done to implement it and discuss any problems with the plan they may have. You will also have to finalise any outstanding issues or concerns at this time.

The fifth session

In practice, this session is normally just a check-up to determine if your clients have responded well to your counselling and this should normally take place after about a month. This follow-up session can also be done over the phone if you believe that your counselling has been successful up to now. The aim of this, your final meeting or contact with your clients, is to make sure that their emotions have quietened down, that their thoughts are under control and if the action steps they put in place have been able to return their day-to-day functioning and lifestyle to normal (more or less).

If your clients are still in distress and showing symptoms after all this time, you will have to refer them to doctors or other counselling professionals for long-term treatment. This can happen if they were under treatment for some disorder before the traumatic incident, or are having a particularly bad time due to the trauma being complicated by other issues such as their grieving over a family member or friend who was possibly killed during the incident.

A final note

It often happens that clients in the later phases of the trauma process come in for counselling. If the worst trauma is past and your clients are not in the *impact phase*, you could have fewer sessions and adjust your approach to match their level of recovery. Unfortunately, such delays in counselling can also lead to major problems.

POST-TRAUMATIC STRESS DISORDER (P.T.S.D)

In my opinion post-traumatic stress disorder (P.T.S.D) is one of the worst mental disorders to have and can cripple a person emotionally for life. Although this is not always the case, people can develop PTSD if they have been exposed to severe trauma, especially for long periods of time, and they either do not receive (or want) counselling at all, or else it is delayed for whatever reason. This typically happens to soldiers during wartime, policemen exposed to frequent violence, or else emergency workers who have been continually exposed to horrendous situations involved serious injuries or death.

These delays happen for a number of reasons, such as counselling not being readily available, being put off for personal reasons such as grieving or the pressure of work, or else simply their believing that they do not need help (cowboy's don't cry).

The most noticeable symptoms are feeling detached from life and other people, being emotionally numb, and being easily irritated and agitated. P.T.S.D can lead to uncontrolled anger and even violence.

Persons with P.T.S.D also have frequent, severe flashbacks, vivid images of the incident(s) which happen all the time and eventually takes over their lives. At night they are prone to nightmares. It can happen to people of all ages and affects their home, social and working lives so badly that in many cases, it can lead to divorce, or no longer being able to find or hold down a job.

The easiest way to see if your client has P.T.S.D is from their history of trauma, the fact that they are anxious and irritated and can even be abusive. They do not normally seek counselling and are usually brought in by a long-suffering spouse, partner or family member. This makes them even more reluctant. As counsellors you are not legally qualified to treat P.T.S.D and the best is to refer them to a qualified medical practitioner, as they will, in all likelihood, need medication.

More information on P.T.S.D falls outside of the scope of this book. However, if you are, or are aiming to become a trauma counsellor or psychologist, do some more research into this disorder.

TRAUMA AND DEPRESSION

Trauma that has not been effectively handled can also cause the person to go into depression. This is the point where they just 'give up' on life as a result of the constant stress and pain from the trauma and withdraw into themselves. Although not as dramatic as PTSD, depression can also badly affect one's home, social and working life. When counselling someone who has been traumatised in the past, be on the lookout for the following symptoms:

This person feels alone, sad or empty and is upset easily. They are prone to very negative thinking and often do not think clearly and logically. This makes them very demanding, what you would call 'high-maintenance'. They have strong feelings of worthlessness and believe that no-one cares. Being with them can be very draining and people usually avoid them, which only makes the matter worse.

Depressed people often withdraw from family and friends and want to be left alone. They complain of being tired all the time, but actually do not sleep well at all. The danger of depression is that their negativity, low energy levels and lack of motivation can eventually lead to their giving up on life and having thoughts of suicide. In fact, depression is one of the main causes of suicide.

It is very difficult to counsel someone who has depression. The easiest way to identify it is if your client has been negative for a long time and does not respond well to your counselling at all, even though you have spent an hour trying to raise their spirits. All I can suggest is that you do not dwell on the past but try to uplift and empower them by finding some meaning and positivity in their lives or in their future. I found that getting them involved in creative hobbies or charity work does help.

At the end of the day it is better to refer a client with depression to a doctor or psychiatrist as they will probably need medication to cope.

BEING CALLED OUT TO A SCENE

Many counselling centres have trauma counsellors on standby on a twenty-four hour basis to do call-outs to the homes or places of work of trauma survivors. Sometimes these teams can also be called upon to do debriefing and counselling for groups of people involved in traumatic incidents, such as armed robberies at banks, malls and stores, as well as fatal factory accidents or even the unexpected death of a co-worker or colleague. This can be very demanding, as members of the team have to stop what they are doing and travel as quickly as possible to attend to the scene.

Sometimes call-outs can also happen in the early hours of the morning and involve travelling to distant outlying areas. For this reason a male and a female counsellor usually form a team, and in this way, also provide for the counselling of both men and women. As you can imagine, it will need many counsellors on standby at different times to offer a twenty-four hour service.

There also needs to be clear guidelines as to when to call out a team and when not to, as in some cases, a trauma counselling team may not meet the immediate need. For example, if the traumatic incident has resulted in injuries such as someone being shot or injured in an incident, accident or disaster, the caller should be told to call the ambulance and law enforcement authorities first and the counselling team should follow up to see if and when they will be needed. Remember that a person has to be awake and able to communicate for counselling, and if they are unconscious, severely injured or sedated, counselling will not be the immediate option. In such cases the team should rather wait until the injured person has been taken to hospital and is able to talk before visiting and offering them trauma counselling. This also applies in the case of a possibly lethal overdose of tablets, in which case you would need to get their address as soon as possible and get an ambulance to their home before activating the team.

In the case of violence a trauma team is also not the first option. For example, if someone is at the scene with a gun or other dangerous weapon (the perpetrator) and poses a threat to the team. Counsellors are not trained or empowered to deal with violence, and once again, the authorities must be called in first to remove the danger before the crisis team is activated.

What usually happens is that the team works under the direction of a supervisor who is called by law enforcement or hospital authorities (or a manager in the case of a company) and told about the incident. The supervisor assesses the need, the appropriateness and the danger to the team, and only if he or she decides that a crisis team would be helpful, will the team be asked to travel to the scene.

If the counselling centre builds a good working relationship with law enforcement and medical agencies, the ideal solution would be for them to contact the supervisor when there is a traumatic incident that needs attention. The supervisor will then only mobilise the team when the call-out is appropriate, the scene safe and the client ready for counselling. If the incident has taken place in an unsafe or even dangerous area, the team must be accompanied and protected by law enforcement officers.

CHAPTER TWO

TRAUMA COUNSELLING ETHICS

As a trauma counsellor you have a great responsibility to your clients and literally have the power to save or destroy a life during your counselling process. Even if you are only a lay-counsellor, you must act responsibly and with integrity at all times.

There are a number of important ethical issues that you must keep in mind when counselling:

BEING CONGRUENT

We all colour our counselling processes with our own states of mind, personal issues and bad past experiences. This means that we have to be *congruent* when counselling, which is being balanced and resilient. In other words, do not be flustered or put off by what your clients have to say and 'keep it together' no matter what happens.

In order to do this, you will need regular up-skilling and debriefing by other counsellors to prevent you having problems such as burn-out and *vicarious trauma*. This can happen regularly, as you often have to deal with horrendous situations, especially if you are doing crisis call-outs or on-site trauma work. If you develop what is called *secondary traumatic stress*, you may also begin to have trauma symptoms. The onus therefore rests on you to seek help if you feel that your ability to do proper trauma counselling is being affected in any way.

KEEPING MATTERS CONFIDENTIAL

When counselling, especially trauma work, you are bound by the same rules of confidentiality that apply to all the helping professions. Traumatised clients are very vulnerable and should always feel secure and protected. This means that you need to inform them that you will keep everything confidential otherwise they may not feel free to share their trauma.

If you reveal confidential information about a counselling session to friends or family, or, if you are counselling company employees and you report delicate details to company management, you are abusing your clients' trust, and this could be bad for them as well as your own reputation.

If you are volunteering at a counselling centre they may want written reports on your clients for statistical reasons. In this case your report should be an outline of the process you followed and should not have intimate details that the client shared with you in trust. However, some counselling centres run supervised trauma counselling programmes in which you are monitored by registered psychologists. In this case you would be allowed to share detailed information with the supervising psychologist, as well as when you refer your clients to other professionals for long-term treatment.

HAVING A STRONG SENSE OF RESPONSIBILITY

Badly traumatised persons in the *impact* phase of trauma are very vulnerable. This places great responsibility on you as a trauma counsellor and means that you have to take the utmost care to ensure that your clients are not *re-traumatised* and are given your best possible attention and treatment. 'Reliving' the event can undo all the good work that has been done and cause their symptoms to get worse, and you have to do all in your power to prevent this. I will give you guidelines on how to avoid this later in the guidebook.

This high sense of responsibility is not only necessary in the case of clients in the impact phase. You will need to take a responsible and professional approach to trauma counselling at all times. This means making sure that your training is up to date, as 'up-skilling' is necessary to improve your counselling skills. Being responsible also means you are on time for your sessions and that you are feeling competent to deal with the powerful emotions. Rather do not do counselling if you are sick or very upset, have been drinking, or are on strong medication, as you need to be fit and able to offer a good service at all times.

BEING TOTALLY NON-JUDGMENTAL

Do not pass any judgements on your clients during trauma counselling and they should always be given your unconditional positive regard. This is especially important in cases where your clients are blaming themselves or feeling guilty by thinking that they were somehow responsible for the incident, could have avoided it, or should have acted in a more positive way. If they sense any type of rejection or judgement from you, this can only add to their distressed state of mind.

You also need make sure that none of your own fixed beliefs, assumptions, biases or prejudices affect your attitude towards them as well as your counselling approach. This means that your clients' religious and spiritual beliefs and moral values should always be respected even if they differ from your own. Your clients are unconsciously (or consciously) looking at your reactions and reading your body-language and you should set aside your own feelings on any matter during the session in order to show that you are totally non-judgemental.

It can happen that your clients ask your opinion on some matter, something which could be taken up as a judgement. When this happens it is best to avoid or deflect the questions by diplomatically pointing out that it is their own feelings and beliefs that are important and not yours.

BEING FLEXIBLE

Being 'directive' means leading your clients in a direction which you think would be helpful. During trauma counselling it is important to quickly identify any unhelpful self-talk and beliefs to stop the destructive cycle of negative thoughts and feelings causing their distress. This does mean that you will have to lead them in isolating their unpleasant thoughts and emotions.

However, if your clients are in the *impact phase* and in great distress, you should allow them the freedom to vent and release these emotions in their own time without any pressure, while you only reflect and empathise. Later on, when they are more composed you can guide them in challenging these negative perceptions or self-talk.

STAYING WITHIN YOUR CLIENT'S FRAME OF REFERENCE

It is important when deciding on your approach to stay within your client's frames of reference. This means considering each clients' conditions at home, finances, beliefs and value systems, coping mechanisms, capabilities and competencies. This is especially important later on when you help them explore options and ways of dealing with their pressing issues and to return a sense of control and mastery to their day-to-day lives. You simply cannot impose or even introduce possible solutions which are not within their capabilities.

BEING COMMITTED

Traumatised clients in the *impact phase* will always need your special attention and extra support. This commitment means that you need to follow important rules during your counselling sessions.

For example:

Always turning up and being punctual

Always turn up and be on time for a counselling session. If you cannot make it at the last moment for any reason, make sure that another counsellor is available to take over your obligation.

Not stopping your counselling once you have begun

Do not allow your counselling session to be interrupted, stopped or cut short for whatever reason. Once your clients begin sharing intimate details, painful emotions and distressing thoughts, they are very vulnerable and stopping your counselling could leave them in a worse state than before. To make sure that you do not have interruptions, do your counselling in a private place or room in which you will not be disturbed. .

Here are a number of easy-to-remember guidelines which you can follow:

- If you think that you will not be able to finish the counselling session due to the available time, or do not have a suitable place for counselling, or feel that you may be disturbed, rather wait a while and plan it for later. This often happens at the scene of an accident or incident when police and emergency services are attending to traumatised persons. In these cases just stay with them, offer support and kind words and reflect feelings until you have the opportunity for proper counselling.

- Once you have begun in-depth counselling you should not stop unexpectedly, as this will leave your client(s) even more upset than before. If you are interrupted by concerned bystanders, friends or family, you should respectfully tell them that you are busy with a trauma counselling session and they should be asked to wait until it is over, unless of course, your clients ask them to be present for extra support as well.

- Do not allow disturbances and interruptions if you are doing counselling at a proper counselling centre or at their work-places. Ask someone to act as a 'gatekeeper' to stop any intrusions.

Language issues

Sometimes English is not the clients' first language and you may have problems communicating and doing your counselling. In this case it is better to refer them to another counsellor who speaks their language rather than to offer an unsatisfactory service. Having a translator to help may work in emergencies, but it is not the ideal solution.

TAKING YOUR CLIENT'S REAL-LIFE SITUATION INTO ACCOUNT

When counselling, you need to take your clients' real-life situation and state of mind into account. For example, if your client is female, a victim of rape and in the impact phase, her emotions will still be raw and she may not wish to share intimate details with a male counsellor, who may remind her of her attacker. It this case, it may be advisable for a lady counsellor to attend to her.

However, the male counsellor can always ask for another woman, a lady counsellor, female friend or family member, to be present during the counselling session. This will help to make sure that she is comfortable in sharing personal information and also help to avoid misunderstandings that may arise, such as the (male) counsellor being accused of inappropriate words or touch.

I have found that if the rape trauma is in the distant past, most women will not mind speaking to a male counsellor, especially over the phone, where the contact is less personal.

WATCHING OUT FOR ROLE-CONFLICT

If you are employed as a staff counsellor by a large company you may have a dilemma if one of the employees need trauma counselling and the company insists on feedback about the session.

This could lead to a breach of counsellor-client confidentiality.

You must remember that first and foremost, you are bound by a pledge of confidentiality and have ethical responsibilities towards your clients. However, the company may need information such as the reason for the employees' state of mind or absenteeism or a recommendation on their ability to perform their duties.

There is a possible solution to this dilemma:

You can inform the employees beforehand that some feedback will have to be given to company management and get them to agree to this. In this case you will need to assure them that personal and confidential details will not be given out, only an outline of the problem and recommendations.

SETTING PERSONAL BOUNDARIES

Traumatised persons are very vulnerable and it can unknowingly happen that some of your clients become overly attached to, or even dependent on you. This can be a serious problem if they find out your personal details such as your home telephone number or address and begin to call you at all times during the day or even at night.

Clients are clients and not friends. It will be best for you to avoid such problems by always insisting on a professional relationship with your clients and that they should not have your personal (home) contact information. Even if it is flattering, do not encourage them to call you all the time.

This problem applies to part-time or volunteer (lay) trauma counsellors. If you are a professional social worker or working for a hospital, department or counselling centre which offers long-term, twenty-four hour service and ongoing support, this would not be such an issue. However, even if you are a professional I would certainly encourage you to set boundaries for personal contact with your clients, such as only being available at the office.

REMEMBERING YOUR ROLE AS A (LAY) COUNSELLOR

You need to know and understand your own role as a lay-counsellor or volunteer.

For example, if, for whatever reason, you are not able to come to the centre or do counselling for a client (or clients in the case of group counselling), inform your supervisor. If necessary, make the arrangements for them to be counselled by another suitably-trained counsellor, yourself.

Secondly, if, after a few sessions, you find that your clients are not responding to counselling and still showing signs of trauma, refer them immediately to a doctor or clinical psychologist. It may be that they have developed either *acute traumatic stress disorder* or P.T.S.D and need to be treated with medication.

Medical issues always become worse after a traumatic incident. Decide early whether you have to refer your clients for medical care.

Boundaries that you need to watch out for:

Male counsellors need to be especially careful when working with female clients to make sure that comforting actions such as hugging or holding their hands are not seen as sexual advances and therefore unethical. You will see that this becomes an even bigger problem if the trauma is linked to a rape or sexual assault by a man.

In the case of men, I would normally advise you not to touch at all, but if a female client has an emotional breakdown and you believe it important to comfort her, simply place your hand on her shoulder or back as she leans forward. Touching is not a problem for lady counsellors, and I have often seen them hugging their distraught clients.

Emotional distance

As a trauma counsellor you always need to be empathetic, but at the same time, learn to keep a healthy *emotional distance* and not allow yourself to be 'pulled into the pit' with your client. You need to keep your own emotions in check when dealing with clients. This is explained more fully in the later section on *vicarious trauma.*

Taking on too much responsibility

Finally, never take away the task of your clients to make and act on their own decisions as this will only further disempower them. Rather strive to *empower* by encouraging them to take the right steps to achieve mastery of their own situations. Badly traumatised clients may need practical assistance with arrangements such as transport or legal matters, but this should rather be left to family, friends or administrative staff and is not your responsibility.

AVOIDING TEMPTATIONS

Finally, you should be careful that you do not succumb to the temptation of abusing your clients' trust for your personal benefit. Traumatised persons are very vulnerable and open to suggestion. If you exploit this vulnerability in order to form business or sexual relationships with them you are acting unethically and this is unacceptable. A sexual liaison with a trauma victim can result in even more major emotional damage and will certainly ruin your reputation as well as the credibility of your counselling centre. Stay professional in your dealings with your clients.

CHAPTER THREE

STRIVING FOR AN IDEAL TRAUMA COUNSELLING ENVIRONMENT

ON-SITE TRAUMA COUNSELLING

If you are on a call-out and at the scene of an incident, disaster or crime, you should try to find a private, safe and reasonably quiet environment for trauma counselling.

If it is an emergency and you want to help immediately, but the conditions are not ideal (such as the scene of an accident), simply give support by touching, listening, reflecting and comforting. However, do not begin with deeper counselling until you have some privacy and control over the situation. It will be worse for your clients if you begin counselling and then have to stop halfway because they are being taken away for medical attention or by the police for questioning.

If you have been called out to the scene of a traumatic incident or disaster and are part of a team, the emergency services will normally find you a reasonably quiet and safe area and set it aside for your counselling. Make sure that access to this area is controlled by gatekeepers. Most airports have special areas for this purpose. And banks, shopping malls or other centres should also be able to provide you with suitable facilities.

If you are part of an employee support programme, or your counselling centre has an arrangement with businesses for trauma counselling for their workers, then your counselling will most likely be on-site at their offices, the factory or their place of work and involve more than one person. This often happens in the case of armed robberies at businesses or the death of a work-colleague as the result of an accident or violent crime.

In this case, it may be best to start by debriefing the traumatised workers as a group and once you have noted those who are badly affected and need special attention, arrange with the manager for them to see you one at a time in a suitable office.

SETTING UP A TRAUMA COUNSELLING ROOM

Arrange your trauma room so that it is quiet, private and has comfortable furniture. Try to avoid a place where there will be interruptions and high levels of noise. If you are in a warm country, make sure you have an air-conditioner, and in a cold climate, heaters, as heat or cold can be an irritation and a distraction and affect counselling. It is also not a good idea to have desks, tables or other furniture placed between you and your clients, as you need to be close enough to offer them practical support. Also keep the colour scheme subdued and avoid bright colours which can affect the mood of the trauma room.

THE CORRECT COUNSELLING POSITION

The ideal position for counselling is for you to sit at an angle to your clients at a distance of about one to one-and-a-half metres. This gives you the opportunity to use your peripheral vision for reading body-language, but also allows for their *personal space*. Personal space is that distance with which one feels comfortable when sitting close to another person. This distance depends on culture as well as the relationship between the two people. For instance, family members will sit closer to one another than strangers without feeling uncomfortable.

This distance of one to one-and-a-half metres is also close enough for you to lean forward and give clients support if they become distressed. Actions such as a reassuring touch or hand on the shoulder, arm or wrist are usually fine. However, if you are a male counsellor, be careful when you are dealing with a female client, as a wrong touch could sometimes be misconstrued as flirting.

I find that ladies will generally not feel threatened by a hand on their upper arms or shoulders, or on their backs if they are sobbing and leaning forward with their head in their hands. But anywhere else could be a problem.

NOT TAKING NOTES DURING FACE-TO-FACE COUNSELLING

I know that many professionals do take notes when seeing clients. However, as a lay counsellor, try not to do this during face-to-face trauma counselling. These sessions can be intense and you need to give your undivided attention to your clients. Sometimes taking notes may also be seen by your clients as breaking confidentiality and lead to their becoming concerned and even suspicious. This will affect your counselling relationship, especially if you are dealing with employees of a company who may think that the notes are for management.

If you have to keep notes or give reports, rather wait until after the counselling session when the client has left the room and then complete them. However, if you are doing counselling online or over the phone it would be fine to take notes, as long as you don't become distracted.

CHAPTER FOUR

SKILLS YOU WILL NEED FOR TRAUMA COUNSELLING

OBSERVING CORRECTLY

Reading and understanding non-verbal communication

The idea behind non-verbal communication is that our bodies reflect the changes in our mental states or emotions by making involuntary movements as well as showing other visible cues. These movements and cues can easily be understood if you have been trained to see them.

This skill is very important and useful during in-person or face-to-face trauma counselling, as it will help you to track and respond immediately to any shifts in the mental or emotional state of your clients. By reading non-verbal cues you will also be able to identify what are called *areas of resistance*, which are those painful thoughts and parts of the story that your clients would like to avoid. In other words, their non-verbal responses to your questioning can show you where the real pain and trauma lies.

You will need to combine a number of skills in order to be successful in reading body language.

THE A-B-C OF BODY-LANGUAGE

'A' IS FOR AWARENESS

Firstly, you need to be fully aware during the session and immediately note any bodily changes taking place during the interaction between you and your clients. This ongoing awareness is called *'being fully present'*.

At the same time you also have to notice the way in which they are using words, as certain words are more emotionally-loaded than others and suggest strong feelings. This also applies to their tone of voice. However, as involuntary movements and shifts can also be due to other factors. These factors as well as the rules for interpreting non-verbal messages are explained later.

'B' IS FOR BODY-LANGUAGE

Reading body-language can be very useful during face-to-face counselling. If you are working online or counselling over the phone, this will not be possible and a lot of information will be lost. However, we will discuss other ways of 'filling in the blanks' when on the telephone a little later on.

In order to read body-language you have to know how and what to look for:

Using your peripheral vision

For instance, you have to practice a new way of observing clients. You need to learn to use your *peripheral vision*. This involves looking out of the corners of your eyes to see the subtle changes in body position and orientation. In other words, do not focus directly on your clients' faces or any body parts in particular, but learn to relax your eyes until they are slightly out of focus and turn your head a little to one side. This allows you to see their entire body, although not clearly, and is why sitting at an angle to clients is useful. Using peripheral vision also allows you to drop your gaze from time to time, as you should not be 'staring down' traumatised clients. This could make them even more uncomfortable and result in changes in body-language which you are causing.

Looking for sudden shifts

The idea of reading body-language is to notice any sudden shifts in your clients' body-positions, body-orientation or bodily tension that are happening during your counselling. If there are no other apparent reasons for this, any sudden change in body-language will suggest that your clients are feeling a new emotion as a result of some thought, idea or mental image they have just had, or are responding with emotion to a statement you have just made, or a question you have asked. This will suggest that that you have reached through to a hidden area of pain or trauma, and if you explore these areas, you will discover the thoughts or memories that are feeding the trauma.

Are there not other reasons for the changes?

If your clients are uncomfortable or distracted by something other than their thoughts and feelings during the counselling session they could also become fidgety, shift around in their chairs and change their body position. This can be very misleading for you as the counsellor trying to interpret changes in body-language. Always make sure that their discomfort is not caused by other factors.

For example, your clients' chairs could be hard and uncomfortable, causing them to shift around trying to find the most comfortable position. The counselling room itself may be too cold or too hot, causing them to be distracted and fidget. Constant interruptions by other people popping into the room will distract and could even annoy your clients. Interruptions could also be due to noise or people talking loudly outside the counselling room. This could make them tense or uncomfortable if they believe that the counselling process, which is supposed to be private and confidential, could be disturbed at any time.

Then there is the question of personal space. Sitting too close to clients could also make them feel uncomfortable. You may unwittingly enter their personal space and this can lead to them changing their body-positions in order to cope with your unwanted closeness. Stay at least a meter away from your clients unless you are physically comforting them.

You need to manage your counselling room so that you eliminate the possibility of interruptions, noise or extreme temperatures.

THE RULES OF BODY-LANGUAGE

In order to correctly read body-language you have to follow the rules:

Viewing body movements as a whole

Articles have been written about small actions such as scratching one's head or pulling one's ear having a specific meaning. This is really not the case. The reason for my saying this is that you will find that non-verbal messages occur as *clusters* of responses and a number of different body parts are active at the same time. The movements also usually occur together with other types of cues. This means that you have to interpret all your clients' body movements as a whole, as well as look for matching changes in their voices and facial expressions before deciding on what are the most likely feelings they are experiencing. By using your peripheral vision you will be able to see their whole bodies, although it may be slightly out of focus, and even small movements can be seen.

Noticing what is being discussed when the body-changes take place

It is very important to look at the *context* in which the changes in body-language are taking place. What part of the traumatic incident is being discussed and what specific words, thoughts, ideas are 'cueing' the body responses? Knowing this will show you those areas that will need special attention during your counselling process.

The shifts and changes you are trying to see will be in their posture, orientation, muscle tension, facial expressions and tone of voice. The cues will all occur together in many cases, and you need to look for the correct combination of body, facial and voice changes that will all point to the same conclusion about this new thought or emotion.

EXAMPLES OF BODY LANGUAGE

There are very definite ways in which your clients' bodies will react to sudden images, emotions and thoughts. These changes will be seen in their body postures, orientation, tension and facial expressions.

Changes in body-posture

Typical changes to your clients' body-posture will be that they either open or close the front of their bodies depending on whether the thought or feeling is pleasant or unpleasant. What this looks like can be explained by imagining a line down the front and centre of their bodies. It is this line that will either be covered up or exposed when a shift takes place in an emotion or state of mind.

Covering up usually involves them folding their arms, crossing their legs, dropping their heads and avoiding eye contact. Badly traumatised clients may even sit on the chair with their legs up against their chests, or if you are counselling them at their homes, lie on the bed in a foetal position. You should also see a change in their facial expressions and possibly even their voices at this time, as part of the cluster of cues. They will certainly look very unhappy and in distress.

A defensive posture such as covering up means that your clients feel *threatened or uncomfortable* by something you have asked them (a question), or have said, or an unpleasant thought or image just entered their minds. This would most likely happen when they are asked to remember details of the traumatic incident.

When this happens, try to change the non-verbal message into words in your mind. For example; 'You have just said something which makes me feel threatened', or 'I have just thought of (or felt) something which has really upset me'. Gently question them further around the issue you were exploring at the time. This is probably an area of resistance, a particular part of the story that is very painful and difficult to share. If they are not ready to open up at that time, just move on and remember to come back to this part again when your client is stronger.

Finally, make sure that the change is not due to their being too hot or cold or uncomfortable before you jump to conclusions.

On the other hand, clients who are defensive in the beginning, but after a while open up their body centres by uncrossing their arms or legs and start to give you attention, are beginning to relax and to trust you. If changed into words, this non-verbal message would be; 'I now trust you enough to expose my vulnerabilities (body) to you'. This opening of the body during the counselling session shows that you are using the right approach and have been successful in gaining your clients' trust and confidence.

Changes in body-orientation

Think again about the imaginary line along the front and centre of your clients' bodies. Body- orientation means the direction in which their bodies are pointing. Put more simply, the way in which they are facing by turning their bodies to the right or left away from you, or by using their shoulders or arms. This can be subtle, such as a slight movement in which they place a shoulder between themselves and you (the 'cold shoulder') and this is usually combined with other cues such as folding their arms or crossing their legs (a change in body-posture), leaning away, and avoiding eye-contact. This can often happen when you are counselling badly traumatised persons in the early *impact phase.*

This turning of the body away from you is a defensive behaviour which simply means that they feel vulnerable and do not have the courage to face you directly. The very thought of having to share intimate and painful details of the incident is itself threatening, or at least severely uncomfortable for them, and this shows up in their body movements.

If your clients suddenly turn away like this during the session, it could be that you have uncovered a particularly painful emotion or thought, or that they are having a flashback of a painful image linked to the event. In this case, the implied message would be along the lines of; 'I have just thought of something, or you have said something which has upset me, and I need to turn away to regain my composure'. This is very useful for your counselling, as it again points to hidden areas or issues that you should explore further, but once again, very carefully.

Also make sure that their shifting is not due to being uncomfortable because of their chairs, your closeness (personal space) or simply annoyed or distracted by outside noises or temperature.

Some clients in phase two (*the recoil phase*) can also be distrustful, stubborn or unwilling to share and use the same defensive body movement (turning or leaning away) to show this unwillingness. Your task in this case would be to win them over with an empathetic approach and kind words until they turn to face you. If this happens during the session, it means that you have gained their trust and built a good working relationship with them. In this case their subliminal message would be; 'I now trust you enough to face you', or 'I am no longer threatened by you', or 'I welcome your help'.

Tenseness in their bodies

Tension can also be seen in your clients' bodies, usually as shaking, tremors or restlessness. In female clients the most common response seems to be shivering and wringing their hands, and for men, shaking, shuffling their feet or clenching their fists. If they take short quick breaths instead of breathing normally and are sweating, this also suggests that they are very tense and anxious. Remember that these actions are usually seen together with more subtle cues such as unhappy facial expressions, avoiding eye-contact and quick furtive glances.

When questioned about their tenseness, your clients may not even know why they feel that way, and during the counselling it will be important to try to get them to name the emotion they are feeling and describe the fearful thoughts that are milling around in their minds which are giving rise to the tension.

What you need to look for is your client suddenly tensing up during the counselling. When this happens, stop and try to remember what was said or discussed when this change took place. In other words, exactly which part of their story were you exploring when they became tense? A sudden increase in body-tension sends the non-verbal message; 'This experience, or the details which I am sharing with you at this moment, are very stressful and unpleasant'. This cue will once again show you where the pain and trauma lies.

Facial expressions

There is nothing better for identifying emotions than your clients' facial expressions. Smiles, raised eyebrows and dilated pupils show pleasant emotions such as happiness and joy, while unpleasant emotions such as fear or horror will have the opposite effect, a drooping face, a frown or grimace. There is a unique combination of facial contractions linked to each emotion and with practice it will be relatively easy to identify them. Knowing what specific feelings or combination of feelings your clients are experiencing is useful for counselling, as each emotion has to be dealt with separately later on when you begin empowering your client.

Changes in their voice

This section is especially important for persons who do counselling online or over the phone.

If you listen carefully you will be able to hear the emotion in your clients' voices or tone of voice. A sudden change to a higher pitch could be due to anxiety, such as when you ask a question which makes them feel threatened. On the other hand, a lower and flatter tone of voice is usually means a swing towards negative thoughts and feelings.

If their voices quiver they are most likely feeling a strong emotion, and a gasp or a quick shallow breath suggests that they have just had a sudden, fearful thought or image, or been overcome by a powerful spontaneous emotion.

Look at their facial expressions to confirm what emotion it is. As I said before, if you are not sure, simply ask them what they are feeling.

'C' IS FOR 'CONSIDER THEIR VIEW'

As a counsellor you always have to be aware of how your clients are seeing 'you'. The same rules of body-language also apply to you. You need to know what non-verbal messages and signals you are sending to your clients during your counselling.

For instance, does your body-language show concern, empathy and compassion or simply a lack of interest? Any negative facial expressions and defensive body movements will soon be seen by your clients and this will badly affect your relationship with them.

Even when counselling online or over the phone, make sure that your choice of words and your voice always express your caring and concern.

Evaluate yourself continuously

This means that you have to monitor your approach, body-language, voice and facial expressions to ensure that your non-verbal messages show empathy, unconditional acceptance, interest and concern at all times.

MATCHING SKILLS

Identifying with your clients

I am sure that most of your clients would like to be counselled by someone with whom they can *identify*; who appears approachable and who they believe will be empathetic, accepting and really understand their predicament. If you are not able to identify with your clients, you could have a problem gaining their trust. This issue of trust is very important. For example, a female rape victim may not be able to fully trust a male counsellor who reminds her of her aggressor and it may be better if she is counselled by a lady counsellor. If you are male it is important to check this out with her before you start counselling, as there may be a problem with trust which is really not your fault.

Meeting their needs

You can find ways of meeting the needs and matching the expectations of your clients. One way of doing this is to match their language and level of education. In other words, do not talk 'over their heads'. Use only simple phrases and ideas that they can understand. If clients are not able to speak English, rather refer them to another counsellor who is fluent in their own language and culture. In serious face-to-face cases when such other counsellor is not available, you can try using a family member or friend as an interpreter.

Another important tip is to try to match your clients' *moods*. For instance, it could be very upsetting for traumatised clients to enter a counselling room and be greeted by a counsellor who is laughing and joking. They may easily think that you are not respecting their emotional distress and pain and this can ruin your attempts to form a good counselling relationship.

This does not mean that you have to be all sombre or glum when doing counselling, but just be prepared to adjust your tone of voice to the feelings of your clients and use a kindly, warm and empathetic approach which shows your respect and compassion. Later on, as their moods lift, you can use a more motivational tone of voice and more directive approach.

ATTENDING SKILLS

Supporting your clients

Traumatised clients will need plenty of support and comforting during your counselling session, especially if they are still in the *impact phase*. Begin your support by showing empathy and a non-judgemental attitude. Sometimes, if they are very distressed, you may physically support them and take them to a chair or coach and sit alongside until they feel better.

Between a lady counsellor and female client, hugging is certainly allowed, but if you are a male counsellor you will have to be careful with female clients. The only physical contact from a male counsellor I would suggest is learning forward and putting your hand on their shoulders or arms. If your female client is highly-traumatised and really needs physical support, a good idea would be to ask another female counsellor or one of her friends to hold and comfort her during the session.

It can happen that some clients will not want to be touched, possibly due to having been physically abused or attacked. You will see this in their body-language. If they stiffen, pull away or show any defensive body movements when you reach out, it means that they do not want to be touched. On the other hand, if they sob, put their heads in their hands and lean forward towards you, it could be that they would welcome a sympathetic hug or hand on the arm.

Building rapport

Rapport is when you are able to create an *affinity* between you and your clients which allows them to accept and be quite comfortable with you counselling them. This rapport is very important if you are trying to build a relationship of trust between you and your clients. Having this relationship will make your counselling so much easier.

To build rapport quickly you need to present a positive *first impression* to clients when meeting them for the first time. Their first impression of you, in turn, depends how you first approach them, what you do or say initially, how closely you identify with them, and if they can see and hear empathy and concern in your tone of voice, your choice of words and body-language.

This means that you have to be very careful at the beginning of the counselling session when you are trying to build rapport, as using harsh words or showing disinterest by means of your body-language will be noticed and they will be less willing to share their trauma with you.

A good first approach is to immediately show concern for your clients by meeting them at the door and taking them to their seats or chairs, as badly traumatised persons are often disorientated and confused. They also feel alone and vulnerable which means that they may even seem withdrawn and not willing to be counselled in some cases. This could happen especially in phase two of the trauma process, when they often just want to be left alone. So put your clients at ease as soon as possible by giving them your first name and quickly create a '*safe space*' for them to feel valued and accepted.

For example: '*Hi Susan, my name is Jimmy. I am a trauma counsellor and I am here to help you through this every step of the way*'

When you are building rapport and the important counselling relationship, you need to understand your clients within their own *frames of reference.* Each person has a 'lens' or specific outlook on the world which they have put together from their past learning experiences and their particular set of beliefs, values, cultures and customs. This affects the way they each process the traumatic experience. Understanding this will give you greater insight into their real emotions as well as their thoughts and states of mind.

This also means that, during the time that you spend with them, you have to put aside your own personal issues, beliefs and views and work with what is acceptable or possible for your clients in terms of their own backgrounds, beliefs and capabilities.

Using small talk

Clients in the *recoil phase* often use coping mechanisms such as *withdrawing* and just want to be left alone. In other words, some of them may be reluctant to come for counselling and will have to be brought in by family members of friends. In such cases, you will have to spend even more time helping them relax until they are willing to share their stories and experiences.

It is also not a good idea to begin immediately with the actual counselling. Remember that you first have to build rapport and some relationship of trust before your clients will be comfortable to speak openly to you. A good way of helping them relax at the beginning is to first engage them in a few minutes of small talk. This means asking them about themselves using non-threatening questions such as; Where do you work?', 'Are you married?, 'Do you have children?', Did you find the place easily?' and 'Who brought you to the counselling centre?'. In other words, *small talk* is a very light type of conversation you can use until they are visibly more relaxed.

It is also important that you do not rush into your counselling. If you have the time and facilities, you could even offer clients tea or refreshments to delay the process until they have settled down. Having a relaxed approach like this, with time for small talk, gives you the opportunity to quietly assess them to see how badly they are traumatised and what phase of the trauma process they are in. Knowing this will be useful to you when you actually begin counselling.

It can happen that badly traumatised clients in the *impact or acute phase* may not respond to small talk at all, as they are totally overcome by powerful emotions. That is fine, and in such cases it will be better to give them plenty of support and reassurance and begin reflecting and acknowledging their feelings immediately.

Helping them to relax

This immediate support could include helping them to relax before you begin with the counselling. Badly traumatised clients are also very anxious and tense. And if you can't seem to get through to them, ask them to try some deep breathing and relaxation exercises. These are discussed in detail in the section on empowerment skills.

'Normalising' their responses

Once they have settled down, begin a support process called '*normalising responses*'. This means re-assuring them that what is happening to them is quite normal and to be expected under the circumstances. This allows them to 'own' their intense feelings and desperate thoughts and not believe that there is 'something wrong' with them.

In the *impact phase* your clients will show intense emotions such as horror, fear, helplessness, guilt and self-blame. Acknowledge each of these feelings in turn and assure them that this is perfectly normal in the case of trauma. They may also be disorientated, con-fused and unable to concentrate on what you say. Once again, use an empathetic approach to let them know that this is fine and that you are with them every step of the way.

During the *impact phase* your clients will most likely also complain of pain, headaches, nausea and diarrhoea. Explain to them that this is also normal and they should not be too concerned. However, they should consult a doctor to help with these symptoms. You also need to inform them to expect that any medical conditions they have, such as high blood pressure or heart problems, could get worse for a while.

If they are in the second (*recoil*) phase, they could also talk of very high levels of stress, tension, irritability and having a short temper. Some of these responses could be new to them and give them addi-tional anxiety, so they will need reassurances from you that this is also normal and to be expected. This will assist them to cope.

Examples of reassurances (*normalising*) could be as follows:

'This is normal and happens to almost everyone in such cases'

'*You will be lucky if you do not have these symptoms*'

'Normalising' their responses is usually done during the first session (stage one of the counselling process), but you can also re-introduce it during the final stage of mastery in order to help them understand that their negative feelings and thoughts during this time have been quite normal for someone who has had such a harrowing experience. However, if at the end of the counselling process (five sessions over a time of two to three months) they have not fully recovered and still have medical or emotional issues, you must refer them to a doctor, psychologist or psychiatrist for more long-term and professional treatment.

Noting their body-language while watching your own

Once they are sitting down in a comfortable chair reasonably close to you, face your clients but do not 'stare them down'. You will need to watch your own body-language as well. If your clients read (or misread) your body-language as not being interested in them, they might not be so willing to trust you and share their experiences. The best manner is to lean slightly forward and keep good eye-contact. This will show your focus and attention. Your facial expression should also be one of concern, empathy and understanding.

If you apply the skills of 'attending' properly, you will begin to see positive changes in your clients' attitude and body-language. If they show defensive body-postures early on you will need to spend more time re-assuring and supporting them before you can think of counselling. For example, if at first they are reluctant to talk and have turned their bodies away from you, don't give up. Just carry on talking to them with kindness and compassion. And when they turn to face you, you will know that you have gotten through to them and you can now begin with your counselling.

However, it can also happen that their need for support is so strong that they will immediately start sharing their story with you. This is a positive sign and means that you already have their trust and can begin counselling.

What you are trying to achieve at this early stage is a good rapport with your clients and the all-important relationship of trust.

Choosing your words carefully

Traumatised clients are sensitive to any form of implied criticism as they are very upset, emotional and vulnerable. They will judge your attitude towards them from *what* you say, as well as *how* you say it, especially if you are counselling online or over the phone. When dealing with clients you must be careful not to say anything which they could interpret as critical, judgmental, unaccepting or disrespectful. Your choice of words and tone of voice should always let them know that you care and have empathy and unconditional positive regard for them.

Empathetic and caring words will lessen their anxiety and feelings of helplessness. It will also help to build rapport and a relationship of trust.

Case study

The following is a short case study in which the counsellor uses kind words to show his empathy, acceptance and concern. Joan is very upset after being mugged in the street and threatened with a knife. She has been crying outside the counselling room for a while before the counsellor comes to fetch her. She is vulnerable and he has to guide her to a chair in the room.

Counsellor: *'Are you feeling a little better now Joan? We are very concerned about you.'*

Notice how the counsellor calls the client by her first name. This helps build the relationship.

Joan's body language shows that she is not ready to speak yet. She is still sobbing and struggling to compose herself. The counsellor sees this and once again responds with kind words that show compassion and understanding.

Counsellor: *'Take your time Joan, and when you are ready we will talk further.'*

Remember to combine empathetic words with suitable body movements as well, such as leaning forward and having a gentle and caring facial expression. Your empathetic approach and choice of words will show your client that you care and cement the relationship of trust.

LISTENING SKILLS

Listening is one of the most important skills in trauma counselling and you need to learn to really listen to your clients. This is not the same as listening during normal conversation, when we mostly just listen to what is being said and nod in agreement from time to time.

Listening is active

Listening is actually an active process in which you have to focus intently on what your clients are saying, consider what is being said or implied (very quickly) and give *ongoing feedback* in a number of different ways, depending on the circumstances.

Combining listening with questioning

Aim for a process that moves smoothly. Keep the listening process flowing and your questioning open-ended. Do not turn your counselling into a question-and-answer session by continually asking questions. In other words, allow your clients the time to share their stories and experiences freely without being interrupted. This will allow them to get in touch with their innermost feelings, thoughts and perceptions.

Any questions you ask when 'listening' should only be aimed at keeping the story flowing and, as mentioned, be open-ended. This means NOT asking them questions that only need a 'yes' or 'no' answer.

Open ended questioning

'Tell me what you saw'

'Tell me what you felt at that moment'

'Tell me what you thought when you saw the gun'

I will deal with open-ended questions in more detail in the section on questioning skills.

Creating a safe space for your clients

Earlier on I stressed how important it is to tell your clients that the counselling is totally confidential and thereby build a solid relationship of trust. This aspect of trust and confidentiality creates what we call a *'safe space'*, a time and place in which your clients feel heard and understood and are willing to share intimate details of their traumatic experiences with you.

To keep this relationship strong you must also continually assure them of your concern, empathy and unconditional acceptance. If they feel judged in any way, they could shut down and not want further counselling.

Planning your listening approach

It is important that you plan your counselling approach and listening process. This means noticing early on in which stage of the trauma process your clients find themselves and adjusting your approach accordingly. For example, if they are in phase one (the impact phase), they will most likely be in great distress and very vulnerable and will need a softer approach with the focus on listening and feelings, whereas if they are in phase two you could possibly be more directive and focus on their negative thinking and perceptions.

You will find that the most important and useful listening skills you use in the early stages of the process are *feedback* and *reflection*, which will now be discussed in detail. These will help you to explore, identify and clarify your clients' negative thoughts as well as the crippling emotions which are causing their distress.

Remember that *exploring* means that you need to be thorough and unpack every thought, emotion and image which is troubling them, going through the whole incident step by step, asking them to share their feelings, emotions and thoughts as they do this. You will have to take great care at this time so that they do not relive the experience (see 'emotional distancing').

Giving continuous feedback

Feedback is explained as keeping your clients constantly informed what you are hearing, feeling, sensing or understanding from what they are telling you. This shows them that you are listening, but also that they are being heard and understood. This helps to cement the relationship of trust that you need and prompts them to share even more freely and deeply.

Secondly, feedback can allow you to respond empathetically. Combine your feedback with a body-posture which shows concern. Nodding will also help you to acknowledge what your clients are saying. This is also helpful in building a strong relationship.

Case study

The counsellor is helping John who has lost his wife in a car accident. He is visibly upset and the counsellor sees and responds to this.

Counsellor: *'John, I can see that this has upset you. This must be very painful for you.'*

It is easy to lose the gist of what your clients are saying, as well as to misinterpret what they really mean as they tell their story. Feedback is also useful to *clarify* what they are saying and cut out these misunderstandings.

For example, continuing with the above case study:

Counsellor: *'John, did I hear you correctly when you said that you were not driving?'*

This feedback gives John the opportunity to confirm or rephrase what the counsellor has just said, with the end result that they have the same understanding and will be metaphorically 'on the same page'.

Finally, feedback allows you to comment on clients' non-verbal messages. Sometimes they can mask their true thoughts or feelings by being fearful, shy or unwilling to open to their pain. In these cases you gently inform them what you have seen from their body-language, and through this you can identify issues or areas about which they are reluctant to speak, open up real issues and help them to be more authentic about how they feel and think.

Case study

Jane was robbed in her car by a masked man with a gun. She is very traumatised and afraid.

Counsellor: *'Jane, you tensed up when I mentioned the gun. I can see that this really upset you.'*

Jane: *'Yes, you are right. When I saw the gun I thought I was going to die.'*

Notice how Jane emphasises the gun. This image and the thought that she was going to die will be the point or moment that the trauma kicked in. This will be more fully discussed later.

Reflecting

Reflecting means that you are (metaphorically) holding up a mirror to your clients to show them their own feelings, thoughts or the details they are giving you relating to the traumatic incident. In this case you highlight important words, ideas or thoughts that they are sharing, and at the same time you let them know that you are listening attentively. This can be quite demanding, as it means you have to pay close attention to what they are saying and also what is not being said, and at the same time, look for nonverbal messages.

There are a number of different types of reflection. They vary from simple one-word responses to paraphrasing a number of statements.

Para-language

This is the easiest form of reflection and means just giving verbal cues, one-word answers or short comments at appropriate times as your clients share their stories. The idea is merely to prompt them to continue.

Case study

Let us use the case study of Janet, a single mother who was con-fronted in her kitchen by a knife-wielding man when she got home after work. It seems that the kitchen door had been left open by her children who were in the play room. In this scene the coun-sellor is trying to get the facts straight.

Janet: '*I think I must have left work at about six o'clock*'

Counsellor: '*Hmmmm*'

Janet: '*When I got home the kitchen door was open*'

Counsellor: '*Yes?*'

Janet: '*At that time I did not suspect anything because I knew my children were at home*'

Counsellor: '*I see*'

Support these brief comments by nodding.

As you can see, paralanguage does not really do anything except to let your clients know that you are listening and to prompt them to continue. It is not really suitable for exploring their emotions or thoughts in any depth. It is more applicable when they are sharing facts (such as the short version of the incident), or in the later stages of the counselling process when you are able to rationally discuss issues with them (the stage of mastery).

Key word repetition

These are also short responses to your clients' statements, but they have a bit more content and meaning in that you repeat key words or phrases which will help you identify your clients' emotions and thoughts.

Let's continue with Janet's case:

Janet: '*I was so afraid*'

Counsellor: '*Afraid?*'

By repeating the key word '*afraid*' the counsellor has highlighted one of the emotions causing the distress (fear).

(You will later need to explore this feeling, as well as the circumstances giving rise to it, in more depth). Once again, reflection will encourage your clients to continue.

Janet: '*Yes, I was terrified*'

Counsellor: '*This must have been very traumatic for you*'

Notice how the counsellor is empathetic to what she is saying. Simple one or two-word reflections can't stand alone and you have to combine them with suitable *empathetic responses*. In doing so, you acknowledge your clients' feelings as well as the seriousness of the situation.

Repeating sentences

You can also reflect whole sentences or phrases

For example:

Janet: '*I was so afraid*'

Counsellor: '*You were afraid?*'

Janet: '*Yes, I was terrified*'

In this case the counsellor has chosen to reflect the whole sentence which identifies the emotion, in this case, fear. However, this is still only a repetition of what Janet has said and gives no extra information.

Paraphrasing

As far as reflection goes, paraphrasing is far more complex and means rephrasing your clients' statements, or *what you believe that they have said or implied*, into different words. If you are on target with your interpretation, your clients will accept that they have been fully *understood* and not just *heard*. Paraphrasing can also assist in clarifying their actual meaning, and is also useful in pointing out contradictions in their thinking, or the actual implications of their line of thought.

Case study

James is a teller in a bank that was recently robbed by armed thugs. He was threatened with a gun and told he would be shot if he did not hand over the money. He has had enough of living with this stress, as this is the second time this year that this branch has been robbed.

James: '*I told the manager that after this second robbery I can't work there again*'

Counsellor: '*You told the manager that you want to resign?*'

James: '*No, just that I needed a transfer to another branch*'

In this example James tells that counsellor that he has misunderstood what he (James) has said. In fact, he says that he has no intention of resigning. Getting it wrong is not a problem, as at least the matter has now become clearer.

Other uses of listening skills

You can also use listening skills to identify the parts of the story that are the most painful for your clients. In some cases, they may avoid talking about certain issues or skim over some details to try to avoid distress. Even though it may be difficult for them to share, you will need to open up these issues at some time or another, and the best way to do this is simply to return to those parts of the story from time to time until your clients are strong enough to face them.

EMOTIONAL DISTANCE

Traumatised clients are very vulnerable, especially in the impact phase. As a result, it is important that you understand the skill of *emotional distance* used in trauma counselling. During the listening and questioning process clients are often asked to share sensitive details of what happened and can easily be *re-traumatised*. This can be explained as actually *reliving* the traumatic incident and re-experiencing the crippling emotions, thoughts and images that arose at the moment of trauma.

This often happens when clients in the impact phase are questioned by unsympathetic officials who are not trained in the effects of trauma. For instance, at police stations when statements have to be taken. We must remember that traumatised persons are often disorientated, confused, numb or in shock, and this could be a problem when having to drive to a police station to give evidence. This is why they should get speedy support and be transported where necessary (including to the counselling centre), by a counsellor, social worker, or at least a competent family member.

It is also important for you to ensure that re-traumatisation does not take place during counselling, and you need to place a *buffer zone* between your clients and the original experience otherwise they could once again go through the intense emotions of shock, horror and fear.

Emotional distance also allows them a measure of control during the counselling session, as they now know that it is not expected of them to relive every moment of the horror of the event.

This sense of control is very important, as it works against the feelings of helplessness and loss of control which usually come with trauma.

Emotional distance is also important for trauma counsellors. You have to take care not to have your objectivity affected by your own emotions when dealing with highly traumatised clients. It can happen that, after years of being exposed to horrendous incidents and trauma counselling, some counsellors develop secondary re-traumatisation and they start showing the symptoms of trauma.

This does not mean that you should be detached and unsympathetic, but rather that you remain aware of your emotional states and show empathy, but still make objective and sound decisions.

Note

If the traumatic incident happened in the distant past, or your clients are already in phase three (the recovery phase), emotional distance will probably not be necessary. However, stay aware of changes in your clients' body language or emotional state during questioning, as you may uncover a very painful memory which could bring back the old feelings.

TECHNIQUES FOR USING EMOTIONAL DISTANCE

Priming your clients for questioning

Always get your clients' permission before asking them to share painful thoughts and memories. If they agree to, and are told to expect questions that may be distressing, they still feel in control and not disempowered. This *priming* should be done early at the beginning of the first session.

For example:

Counsellor: *'Is it in order if I ask you a few questions about the incident?'*

Counsellor: *'Would you be willing to share some of the details of the incident with me?'*

Later on, when broaching a particularly painful or highly-emotive area, you can further prepare your clients.

For example:

Counsellor: *'I am going to ask you some difficult questions about what took place'.*

Counsellor: *'If you are not comfortable with answering these questions please let me know'*

Counsellor: *'This is the most effective way of helping you'*

Using euphemisms

Another simple way to lessen the emotional impact effect of questioning is to use *euphemisms* as much as possible.

For example:

Counsellor: *'How many people had passed on, or were gone?'* (instead of 'were killed')

Counsellor: '*Where were the people lying?*' (instead of 'dead bodies')

Counsellor: '*Tell me what happened the night you were hurt*' (instead of 'attacked' or 'raped')

Asking for a shortened version of the incident

Another way of limiting the chances of re-traumatisation and priming your clients for deep sharing is to initially ask for a shortened, purely factual version of events and with no mention of feelings, thoughts or images. In other words, ask your clients to first skim through the incident before they share any intimate details. It has been found that this simple exercise acts as a non-threatening *warm-up* for the more painful sharing of emotions, thoughts and images which go together with a detailed, step-by-step account of what happened.

Case study

Sandra was on her way to work when she was held up at an intersection by a man with a gun.

Counsellor: '*Before we go into all the details, just tell me briefly what happened.*'

Counsellor: '*I understand that you were on your way to work when you stopped at an intersection and a man pointed a gun at you?*'

Sandra: '*Yes, That is correct*'

(Notice the guidance provided by the counsellor to get only a shortened version of the incident)

Using the past tense as much as you can

Notice how I used the past tense when asking for the short version. The past tense can also be used when questioning your clients about the full sequence of events, including their emotions, negative thoughts and troubling images. This sends the subtle message that the incident is in the past and they do not need to relive it again.

Continuing with the case study:

Counsellor: *'At the time that this happened, how did you feel?'* (past tense)

Sandra: *'I was terrified'*

Counsellor: *'And if you think back, what was the first thought that came into your mind?'* (past tense)

Sandra: *'I thought he was going to shoot me.'*

Encouraging your clients to take a third-person view of the incident

When later asking for step-by-step details of the incident, also try to let them imagine that they are telling you a story in the *third-person*. In other words, they should try to recall the incident as if they were observers and see the events as merely passing them by on a screen or through a window. This allows them to take a step back from the actual experience. This is not easy and I think the process is a bit dated. However, if your clients are in a bad state and really reluctant to speak, you could offer them this alternative and see if they are up to it.

Using our earlier case study:

Sandra: *'I really don't feel up to going through the whole incident again.'*

Counsellor: *'I understand'. Let's try another approach. What if you see yourself an observer looking on?' 'What would you see?'*

Knowing and understanding that it is not necessary to actually relive the trauma will help Sandra feel more in control and lessen her chances of returning to the original experience and the feelings of intense fear, terror, horror and helplessness.

Using fantasy narratives (metaphors) when the incident is too painful to recall

If the pain of the memories is too intense and the client does not feel up to sharing intimate details of the incident, you can try using symbolic speech to stand in for the original experience, such as metaphors to veil painful aspects of the story. In other words, in collaboration with your client, build a fantasy narrative that will stand in for or represent the actual traumatic incident (s). This will put an *emotional distance* between the clients and highly distressing details of the event. This should work well with children or adults recalling severe childhood sexual or physical abuse from the past.

Case study of Tina

This is the real-life case study of 'Tina' (not her real name) who could not imagine going through all the painful details of her childhood rape and abuse. Tina responded to a metaphorical approach and was able to use the framework of a childhood fantasy tale to tell her story.

She described her ordeal in trying to come to terms with what happened as that of a knight fighting a dragon. In this case, the dragon was her abuser and her story of abuse, the knight was herself, battling to overcome her past memories. We were able to introduce those who supported her as helpful characters and I was able to pose questions based on the narrative. Everything said had a hidden metaphorical meaning which I was able to interpret without her having to relive the events. This allowed her to tell her story and find some relief without the intense emotions.

Interpreting your clients' dreams and drawings

Another way of using symbols in trauma counselling is to assist clients to interpret their troubling dreams. Disturbing dreams are often associated with trauma. The psychologist Carl Jung believed that dreams are symbolic messages which often point to repressed feelings and unresolved pain. Interpreting your clients' dreams would certainly be a *less-threatening* way to identify and deal with details of the trauma. Guidelines for interpreting dreams fall outside of the scope of this guide, but are in my e-book 'How to Interpret your Dreams' published by Neo-World Consultants (2013).

In the same way, looking at the symbols in drawings done by clients (especially children) can also provide a glimpse into the memories arising from their trauma. This does mean that you will have to do research into this skill in order to be able to interpret the drawings.

ADDITIONAL LISTENING SKILLS

Immediacy

There are a number of other lesser known listening skills that you can also use during counselling. One of these is immediacy. Sometimes your clients can be confused or unaware of what they are actually feeling and may flounder around trying to find the right words. In this case, immediacy is an 'immediate' response or reflection of emotions or thoughts that you believe they may be having as you think about their situation, their use of words and non-verbal messages.

In other words, you translate their use of words, innuendo, tone of voice and subliminal messages, as shown in subtle changes in body-language, into specific emotions and thoughts and reflect this back to them as empathetic responses.

Case study

A young woman, Cathy, has just been accosted in her home and almost raped. She managed to escape by running away but is very traumatised.

Counsellor: '*I can see that you are still very upset*'
(In response to Cathy's body language and visible tension)

Cathy: '*Yes, it only happened a short while ago and I have not yet settled down yet*'

Counsellor: '*You must be feeling quite desperate*'
(In this case the counsellor is 'offering' Cathy an emotion)

Cathy: '*Yes, I am very tense and can't relax at all*'.

Handle this skill with care and make sure that you do not introduce thoughts and emotions that are not actually there, as your clients may simply agree and accept what you are saying without you getting through to the truth of the matter.

Using silence as a tool

Although not a true method of reflection, if used skilfully, purposeful moments of silence can be powerful tools for opening up issues and even hidden areas of pain.

Self-insight and self-examination need moments of reflection, and sometimes we, as counsellors, talk a little too much and rattle off ideas, or our own version of events, without giving the client enough time to explore and consider what they are really feeling, thinking or imagining.

Purposeful moments of silence are very useful during sensitive questioning, especially in cases in which you believe that your clients are either not admitting to some feeling or thought, or else are unaware of how they really feel.

The idea is to consciously introduce a pregnant pause, a quiet moment for them to feel, think and reflect inwardly. You may find that during these moments they uncover powerful hidden emotions or even arrive at new insights or perspectives on the incident.

Sometimes a simple pause is enough to invite your clients to 'feel' and to then share more deeply.

Let us put this in the context of Sandra's case:

Sandra: '*And so when I passed the intersection where the robbery took place I felt so anxious*'

Counsellor: '*All those thoughts and feelings came back again*'
(a few moments of silence)

Sandra takes a deep breath and begins to sob uncontrollably as the feelings come flooding back

Sandra: '*Yes, I remember everything so clearly*'

Try not to keep the pauses too long, or clients may wonder why you are not responding to them. In other words, combine your use of silence with other forms of reflection to keep the process going.

QUESTIONING SKILLS

Reflecting back the information given to you is good for listening but a time comes when you need to explore more deeply. You therefore need to combine *questioning* with feedback and reflection to produce a continuous, smooth process.

Direct your questions at identifying, unpacking and exploring the powerful images, emotions and negative thoughts associated with trauma, as well clarifying details, facts and issues with every step. However, there are a number of guidelines relating to your questions which you must keep in mind:

Open-ended questioning

Your questions, in most cases anyway, should be *open-ended.* Open-ended questions are those which cannot be answered with a simple 'yes' or 'no' and prompt clients to think and share deeply.

You also have to use cue words to indicate what you are looking for.

Remember the case study of Janet who was accosted in her kitchen?

When you question for facts:

Counsellor: '*What happened when you went into the kitchen?*'

Janet: '*I saw a man standing there and he had a knife in his hand*' (fact)

When you question for feelings:

Counsellor: '*What did you feel when you realised there was an intruder?*'

Janet: '*I felt terrified*' (terror)

When you question for thoughts and self-talk:

Counsellor: '*What did you think at that moment?*'

Janet: '*I thought he was going to kill me*'

Open-ended questions invite your clients to share openly and freely without being interrupted. If you do pose closed questions with simple yes-or-no answers you could end up with uncomfortable silences. Too many yes or no answers could even affect the whole counselling process, as you could easily get stuck and not know what to ask next. .

The bottom line here is that counselling should not become a 'question and answer' session and you should only pose yes–or–no questions when you have to.

Using cue words for your questioning

As mentioned, whether you are asking for facts, feelings or thoughts, use cue words to let your clients know exactly what you want. If you want facts, your cue words will be 'what' or 'where'. For example '*what happened then?*', '*What did you do then?*' '*Where did this take place?*'

If you want to know their feelings at the time, use questions with the word 'feeling'. For example: 'What did you feel at the time?', 'What was the feeling?', 'And how did you feel then?'

Using the same approach, if you are wanting to explore your clients' thoughts or self-talk, use the cue words '*mind*', '*thinking*' or '*telling*' and phrase your question in such as way that they clearly understand that it is their self-talk, thoughts or beliefs which you are asking for.

Notice the cue words the counsellor used in Janet's case:

Counsellor: '*What did you think at that moment?*' (think)

This could also be phrased in different ways:

Counsellor: '*What went through your mind all this time?*'

Counsellor: '*What did you tell yourself at that moment?*'

When you are posing these questions remember to make mental notes of what they are telling you, as you will have to explore these facts, emotions of thoughts in more detail later. If you are counselling online or over the phone you can make written notes as you go along.

Only asking relevant questions

During your questioning encourage your clients to share openly and freely. Do not interrupt them with needless questions. Remember to respond with empathy and reflect all their fears and pain as it flows out.

Timing your questions carefully

Do not 'attack' your clients with emotionally-demanding questions right at the start of the session. Use small talk and ask simple questions about their families and work until they have relaxed and are strong enough to deal with more difficult questions on their innermost thoughts and feelings.

You must keep in mind that during the first stage of trauma counselling you are trying to *build a relationship of trust*. If your questions are too threatening and painful *to begin with*, and you have not got their total trust and acceptance, they might shut down.

Also remember to *prime* your clients for difficult questions (let them know that you are going to ask them about sensitive details), and use *emotional* distance if they are still very traumatised. This is usually the case in the Impact phase.

Avoiding leading, loaded or judgemental questions

You can also place your clients under pressure to answer in a certain way by asking them 'leading' or 'loaded' questions. If you lead them in a certain direction they may not be sharing exactly how they feel or what they are thinking.

Also avoid **'why'** questions, as they could feel judged because they did not do what you expected.

These are a few examples of leading, loaded or judgemental questions, and you must avoid them.

Counsellor: '*You want him punished, don't you?*' (leading)

Counsellor: '*So, are you feeling guilty about this?* (loaded)

Counsellor: '*Why didn't you call the police?*' (judgmental)

Handling challenging questions carefully

Traumatised persons are very vulnerable during the *impact phase* and they may have already 'closed up 'to some extent. This is to protect them from the pain, which can be unbearable. You should therefore phrase your questions carefully so as not to upset them further.

When your client is visibly distressed, do not pose challenging questions such as '*What is it that you are not telling me?*' Try to identify and bring their feelings to the surface using other, more gentle techniques such as *reflection* or *immediacy*.

HOW TO USE YOUR QUESTIONING SKILLS

Questioning is there to help you identify, unpack and explore the facts of the incident, as well as to uncover traumatic images, crippling emotions and negative thoughts. Remember to merge your questions with feedback and reflection of their answers to produce a *continuous, flowing* process. Remember to also use open-ended questioning where possible.

Let's go a little deeper into the skill of questioning, as this is an important section. You remember that I mentioned that you need to phrase your questions in such a way that your clients know exactly what you want, using the *key or 'cue' words* to show them what you are asking for. Let us look at a few more examples.

You will recall Sandra's case study in which she was robbed in her car at an interaction by a man with a gun.

Exploring facts

Counsellor: *'Tell me what happened when you entered the intersection'* (details)

Sandra: *'I was on my way home when I stopped at the intersection of Smith and West Streets'*

Exploring images

Counsellor: *'What did you see when he came towards you?'*

Sandra: *'All I saw was the gun'*

Counsellor: *'You saw the gun?'* (reflection)

Sandra: *'Yes, the image of the gun is still in my mind'*

Exploring emotions

Counsellor: *'What did you feel when you saw the gun?'*

Sandra: *'I was terrified'*

Counsellor: *'You were terrified?'* (reflection)

Sandra: *'Yes, I completely froze up'*

Exploring thoughts

Counsellor: *'When you saw the gun, what was the first thought that went through your mind?'*

Sandra: *'I thought I was going to die'*

Counsellor: *'You thought this was the end?'* (reflection)

Sandra: *'Yes, and that I will never see my children again'*

Questioning is also used during the empowerment stage to act against the effects of your clients' negative self-talk (cognitive restructuring). This will be shown later.

CLARIFYING SKILLS

It is very important to be absolutely sure of the facts and of your clients' emotions and thoughts, as you will have to be dealt with each one separately. You also have to know exactly *what happened* during the incident. You must understand that you are dealing with *perceptions*, and their thoughts are likely to be confused and sometimes irrational due to the intense emotions from the trauma. Unfortunately, these perceptions become *reality* to them and it will be important to separate reality from fantasy and truth from negative perceptions which only make the situation worse.

This is called *clarifying* and it can be used during reflection, which, as I have already explained, is when you highlight key words or phrases, especially those which seem confusing, and ask your client to explain, clarify or correct their meaning.

Case study of Celeste

A young wife Celeste returns home to find her husband murdered, lying in a pool of blood.

Celeste: '*Can you imagine what it was like to see him lying there like that?*'

Counsellor: '*You felt afraid?*'

Celeste: '*No, it was more a shock and numbness*'

In this case the counsellor has not correctly named Celeste's emotions, but that is still fine, as he has now clarified what she was really feeling at the time (shock and numbness).

You can also ask for clarification during direct questioning, but use simple phrases to introduce the question. These are called 'lead-ins'.

Here are a few examples of lead-ins:

Counsellor: '*Let me understand you correctly, you are saying ...?*'

Counsellor: '*Just to clarify, you mean that ...?*'

Counsellor: '*Can I just clarify something?*' '*You say your children were not at home when the incident occurred?*'

Finally, there may be facts, feelings, thoughts or issues which are masked or less obvious, but you should be able to infer them from subtle verbal or non-verbal cues given by your client such as the way words are used, innuendo, tone of voice or changes in body-language. Point out these cues and use them to gently probe for more clarity.

Let us again use the case study of Cathy who was sexually assaulted in her home.

Cathy: '*I just want him to pay for what he did*' (verbal cue)

Counsellor: '*You sound angry*'

Cathy: '*Yes, and I believe I am right in feeling this way*'

Counsellor: '*So, just to clarify, you are angry and not afraid about what happened?*

Counsellor: '*Yes, I can see this*' (non-verbal cues)

In this case the counsellor has noticed that her earlier feelings of fear and helplessness have now gone over into anger as a result of what happened. This is a good sign, as it shows the second recoil phase, and if she can redirect her anger, it will help in her healing.

EMPOWERMENT SKILLS

Empowerment means supporting and boosting your clients emotionally and mentally, helping them to let go of negative feelings and self-talk and take on new, more positive and uplifting emotions, thoughts, beliefs and ideas about themselves and their abilities. The purpose of empowerment is to help them to eventually return to a sense of normality and in the long term, mastery of the trauma situation and of their lives.

Helping to return a sense of balance, control and mastery to your clients

A traumatic incident is very stressful and people often have a sense of being alone in a frightening situation, as well as feeling helpless and having lost control of their lives. They can be totally crippled by emotions such as horror, fear and desperation, and later on, also by guilt and self-blame if they begin to believe that they could have avoided the incident or been more proactive in some way. In some cases they may well consciously or inadvertently played a major part in the incident. For instance, regret and self-blame at being the driver in an accident in which someone is killed. Even if they were involved in triggering the incident in some way, your job as the counsellor is not to pass judgement but to support and assist them to deal with the negative thoughts and emotions. These emotions will be reflected in their thoughts and self-talk.

Hopefully you have been successful in helping them to release some of the stress and debilitating emotions in the first three stages of the counselling process and now you will apply empowerment skills in stage four, which should be towards the end of the first, or during the second session. The ideal outcome of empowerment is to be successful in challenging and changing their negative self-talk and irrational perceptions and beliefs for the better and rebuilding their confidence and a sense of control.

Empowerment techniques

In trauma, emotional distress is often set off and later sustained by irrational beliefs and distorted perceptions about themselves and their role in the incident. There are a number of common myths in human thinking such as '*I must be competent and capable in everything I do*' which can result in unrealistic expectations of oneself and lead to feelings of anxiety, self-blame and guilt. As I said, this is especially true when the person feels that he or she could have acted in a more positive, constructive or responsible manner.

During your counselling you should have been keeping mental notes of your clients' emotions, negative thoughts and percep-tions and self-limiting beliefs, as well as of all the circumstances surrounding the incident. During the empowerment stage you will need to use your common-sense, logic and reason to summarise, link and analyse this information and use any positive aspects you see to support and uplift your clients. At this time, each line of negative self-talk and each irrational belief you have identified will have to be considered and challenged.

Praising and supporting your clients

Praise them for their courage in being prepared to work through the whole incident with you. It is very difficult to have to share your pain and feelings with others.

Changing your clients' thoughts and perceptions to reduce emotional stress

You must not challenge your clients' thoughts and perceptions in the *impact phase* of trauma, as they are too vulnerable and they could easily have a setback. Later on, when your clients' feelings and responses are more manageable (stage four), you can begin to use empowerment techniques to challenge any self-defeating thoughts, perceptions and unrealistic beliefs which are sustaining their feelings of helplessness, worthlessness, incompetence, guilt and loss of control. In other words, your focus should be on unpacking (*deconstructing*) and remodelling (*reconstructing*) your clients' self-talk in order for them to reach a more positive understanding and acceptance of their actions during the incident.

We use mostly two techniques during empowerment, *reframing* and *cognitive restructuring*.

Reframing your clients' thoughts and perceptions

Negative thoughts and images from the traumatic incident give rise to powerful emotions as well as a constant replaying of the event. As a result of these emotions, your clients' perspective of the situation will often be distorted. You, as the counsellor, are therefore in a better position to understand the actual circumstances to which your client was exposed and, in most cases, to see that their feelings of guilt and negative self-beliefs are unfounded and nothing but a fantasy.

Unfortunately, their fantasy becomes reality to them, and it your role to reveal the true facts of the matter and offer them a different reality in which their negative thoughts and beliefs are no longer justified. This is the crux of the technique called *reframing.*

Reframing is explained as offering a more objective view of the situation, *alternative interpretations* of what was, or was not possible for your clients to have done during the incident.

This would mean showing them new perspectives which prove that their actions were normal, rational, considered, correct and actually indeed necessary under the prevailing circumstances. And that any other action could have produced a far worse outcome. In this case we assume that these new, more positive points of view will help to reduce feelings of helplessness, loss of control, guilt and self-blame.

EXAMPLES OF REFRAMING:

Helping to remove guilt and self-blame

In many cases trauma clients carry feelings of guilt or self-blame, believing that they could have somehow avoided the situation or coped better in some way by acting differently. In most cases this assumption is not rational or justified. Using the power of hindsight you can review and lay out in a step-by step way, your clients' actions during the incident to show that they acted quite reasonably under the circumstances, and even point out worse scenarios that could have occurred had they acted differently.

Let us go back to the case of Janet who was confronted by a knife-wielding intruder in her kitchen and who now blames herself for not having done more to stop the robbery, such as pushing the panic button. The process could be as follows:

Counsellor: '*What could have happened if you had pushed the alarm button in front of him?*'

Janet: '*There was a good chance he would have stabbed me.*'

Counsellor: '*So by not pushing the alarm button you actually saved your life?*'

Janet: '*I suppose you could say that*'

In this case, the counsellor has shown that her action in not pushing the alarm button while the intruder was right in front of her was the correct one, and that she has nothing to feel guilty about.

Working with 'should have' or 'ought have' self-blame judgements

Our society believes in the myth that everyone must be competent and capable in everything that they do, otherwise they are failures. After a traumatic incident, your clients' actions (or inactions) can place unrealistic pressures on them. Once again, during reframing you can show that the situation could have been even more disastrous if they had acted differently.

To continue with Janet's case study:

Counsellor: '*What could have happened if you had resisted?*'

Janet: '*He said he would kill me*'

Counsellor: '*You told me that he had a knife pointing at you*'

Janet: '*Yes, that is true*'

Counsellor: '*So by not fighting him you actually prevented yourself being killed?*'

In this case Janet survived, and now needs to be shown that this may not have been the case had she decided to act in a different way.

In other words, the ideal outcome of reframing is for your clients to come to a new realisation that what they did was correct under the circumstances and there is no reason for guilt or self-blame.

Reframing can be difficult in cases where your client actually did play a role in the incident, such as being the driver of a vehicle in an accident in which another person was killed. However, your task is to assist your clients and this may mean finding any reason to lessen the impact of their guilt. How this is possible becomes more evident in the next section on cognitive restructuring.

Challenging negative thinking

Cognitive restructuring is a term which simply means changing your clients' negative thinking. The way in which this is done is to challenge and 'refute' any of your clients' self-defeating thoughts or irrational beliefs and replace them with more positive and self-affirming statements.

As mentioned earlier, we are assuming that these thoughts and beliefs are sustaining the intense negative emotions felt by your clients, and by changing these thoughts and beliefs, these emotions should lessen naturally over time.

You can do this in a number of ways:

First, using the information shared earlier by your clients, offer them new insights into their actions which point to the fact that they were not as helpless as they initially believed, and that they acted with reasoning, deliberation and intent. If you are successful, the new insights should enable them to let go of some of the crippling emotions such as feelings of helplessness, loss of control, guilt and self-blame that are dominating their internal self-talk.

Second, using the power of hindsight, you could suggest to your clients that their perceptions of the situation and their role in the incident were coloured by their emotions and are not realistic, not rational or simply not true when viewed objectively. Use real examples taken from their story to justify your point of view. If your arguments are accepted by your clients, they should let go of their negative thoughts and beliefs and be prepared to replace them with more self-affirming self-talk.

The process uses reflection and questioning to break down the negative self-talk into manageable 'chunks':

Case study

Let us use the case study of Peter who was hijacked by a man with a gun, was afraid and simply handed over the keys to his car:

Counsellor: *'What do you regret about your role in the incident?'*

Peter: *'That I should have fought back'*

Counsellor: '*Why was it important of you to fight back?*'

Peter: '*By fighting back I would have proven to myself that I was not a coward*'

Counsellor: '*What are you telling yourself now?*'

Peter: '*That I am a failure as a man and that no-one will respect m*e'

The counsellor isolates segments of Peter's self-talk and sees that his thinking becomes more and more negative with each line of self-talk.

'*I should have taken action*'

'*I failed to take action*'

'*I am a failure as a man*'

'*No-one respects a coward*'

'*No-one will respect me*'

As you can see, what happens in Peter's mind begins as a perception influenced by the common myth of *total competency* I mentioned earlier, and a 'should have' judgement and a lack of belief in himself which he accepts as reality. He now generalises this judgement and begins to reflect negatively on all his abilities, including his integrity and competence. This leads to negative feelings of helplessness, self-blame, a sense of failure, a fear of rejection and ultimately, a *loss of self-worth.*

Using cognitive restructuring you attempt to argue against and break these chains of negative self-talk using the true facts of the situation from the information given to you during the earlier stages of the counselling process. In this, you have the power of hindsight and a reasoning mind which is not affected by emotion, and using these tools, your aim must be to show your clients that their perceptions and beliefs are drawn from a traumatic response and are not reasonable in view of the actual circumstances. In some cases they are simply not true at all when viewed impartially.

Let us go back to Peter's case study

For example, the first line of self-talk is the belief that he *should have* fought back, based on the myth of 'must-have' competency. In this case you highlight the true facts of the difficult situation which he was in.

In hindsight, the facts are that he was alone in the car on a deserted road and under threat of death from a lethal weapon. Realistically speaking, in climbing out of the car and fighting with the hijacker there was a possibility that he may have been able to overpower him, but if he was not, there would have been no going back. A failure to overpower the hijacker would have been fatal. Would any reasonable man have taken that chance? Probably not! It is simply the stress and bad feelings from the trauma that are now prompting him to doubt himself.

Once he sees that his self-talk was triggered by emotion and accepts the new, more reasonable perspective, the first line can be changed (restructured) to fit a more realistic and positive view of himself, for instance;

'I did the best I could under the circumstances'

As a result of this new insight and revised view, the other lines of self-talk should fall away and the feelings of self-blame and failure should soon dissipate.

Stopping their feelings of helplessness / giving them back a sense of control

If there are a number of different emotions at play, changing one line of a string of negative self-talk may not be enough to reduce the clients' traumatic stress, such as in this case study, in which, even if the self-blame is resolved, Peter may still remember the feelings of *helplessness* that he had during the incident. Other episodes of self-talk may therefore have to be challenged and changed.

In our present case study, Peter's feelings of helplessness come from a perceived loss of control that took place, resulting in him merely handing over the keys.

His self-talk in this case would probably be along the lines of: -

'*I was helpless. I just gave him the keys.*'

To challenge this self-talk you will need to show that he was, in fact, thinking rationally during the incident, had acted positively, and had a measure of control over his situation which lessened the seriousness of the outcome. Once again, this would mean that you have to remember, link and summarise any details he gave you earlier.

Once again, if we use the same case study:

Counsellor: '*So by giving the hijacker your keys you got rid of him quickly?*'

Peter: '*Yes, I suppose I did*'

Counsellor: '*So you actually resolved the situation quickly? 'You did very well.'*

If Peter accepts this new insight he could change his negative self-talk to;

'*I was actually not helpless. I was able to get rid of him quickly and keep him from shooting.' 'I was actually in control*'

Showing them the importance of having a plan

Another way of changing negative thoughts and self-talk would be use the idea of 'having a plan'. Some of the self-judging beliefs stemming from the incident may be from the perception of having had no control over the situation. If you can show your clients that they were thinking and actually had a plan of action in mind, and that this plan was able to defuse the dangerous situation, they can regain their sense of control and let go of the idea of being helpless.

Changing their thinking in this way can help them to release their *feelings* of helplessness and loss of control.

Using Peter's case study again, this would play out as follows:

Counsellor: '*So you were thinking of ways to get the hijacker to go as soon as possible?*'

Peter: *'Yes, I suppose I was'*

Counsellor: *'Your plan was to hand over the keys quickly so that he would just go?'*

Peter: *'I suppose I was thinking that'*

Counsellor: *'This tells me that you were thinking all the time.'* *'You were actually in control of the situation and made a conscious decision'*

Peter: *'I never looked at it that way'*

A new, positive thought like this can change Peter's earlier belief that he was helpless to another which suggests *competence*, allowing him to rebuild his shattered self-esteem.

Trying to reach a turning point in the counselling

This could be the *turning point* for Peter, the moment of realisation at which he would come to understand and accept more positive insights about himself and his actions and be able to change his negative self-talk. Hopefully he will also now be able to let go of some of his feelings of fear, helplessness, guilt and self-blame and the idea of being a helpless victim and begin to see himself as a courageous survivor of a very difficult situation.

Ideally, being successful with changing your clients' self-talk (cognitive restructuring) should help to remove the thought-basis causing or sustaining the unpleasant feelings normally associated with trauma, but sometimes other techniques are also necessary, especially to relax the body.

Other empowerment skills

These other exercises focus directly on lessening the effect of the trauma on the body itself. They can be used at any stage of the process to lower your clients' tension levels and help them to relax. These breathing and relaxation exercises are especially useful for clients in the impact phase.

Breathing and deep muscle relaxation

This is a relaxation exercise that allows your clients let go of troubling thoughts and bodily tension. Guide them through the process yourself using a quiet tone of voice.

Ask your clients to close their eyes, sit quietly and begin to breathe deeply and regularly. After a few moments they should then begin to imagine a wave of peace slowly moving up from their feet, though the muscles of their ankles and legs, into their hips, over their chests and up their backs. At the same time, ask them to empty their minds of all thoughts until it is completely quiet.

Tell them not to use willpower to force their thoughts out, as this only creates new tensions. They must just relax and allow their thoughts to gently pass in and out of their minds without giving them any attention. The idea is for their brain activity to just slow down until they are is just 'ticking over' without any thinking taking place.

They should also set their minds on feeling more and more peaceful as the 'wave' passes through each muscle, limb or organ. Finally, guide them to imagine the feeling passing up their necks and out the top of their heads. At the end of the exercise ask them if they feel any better. If not you can do the exercise more than once, and each time ask them to rate how they are feeling.

A relaxing meditation

I know that some people are not happy with meditation. However, this particular meditation is only an exercise to relax the body and does not have any religious meaning. Meditation is actually also based on sound psychological principles such as mental relaxation, mental creating and conscious mind control and studies have shown that it can bring about positive changes to one's brainwave patterns and tension levels. In fact, it has become a recognised practice in some forms of therapy, including trauma.

The following is a simple meditation to release the tension caused by trauma. You can either guide your clients through it during your counselling sessions or let them do it at home or at the office.

Your clients must sit quietly and comfortably, close their eyes and begin breathing to a slow count of one to five. They must focus on nothing else but the counting (either aloud or in their minds).

This would be the process if you are guiding them. Breathe in 1,2,3,4,5, hold your breath, 1,2,3,4, 5, breathe out 1,2,3,4,5, hold your breath 1,2,3,4,5, breathe in 1,2,3,4,5, and so on.

They must carry on with the counting and breathing until their minds have become quiet and they feel more relaxed. They then report on each cycle of this meditation and rate how they are feeling on a scale of one to ten. Look for an improvement in their tension levels.

Visualisation

Visualisation can be explained as creating scenes in our minds using our imagination. This is also a good way of dealing with the tensions and stress from trauma and works like this; we know that our subconscious minds have a lot to do with regulating our heart-rate, blood pressure and body tensions and it has been shown that it (the subconscious mind) cannot always tell the difference between an imagined and a real-life experience. For example, think of the nightmares we have all had where we woke up sweating and with our hearts pumping. In other words, if we do it properly, a visualised (imagined) experience can affect our bodily responses.

The simplest exercise in this case is to simply guide your clients through a process of creating peaceful scenes in their minds, such as their 'happy place', the beach, a holiday or nature scene, a place where they would normally relax, and check their tension levels after each exercise. Find the one that works best and ask them to do this regularly.

A more advanced form of visualisation would be to ask your clients to visualise a better outcome to a particularly traumatic scene from their narrative or story. In other words, to recall a scene from the trauma incident in which they were fearful and now visualise the same scene, but this time see themselves as strong and unafraid. They do not have to change the outcome, just the feeling.

For example, in the case of Janet, she would still see herself facing off against the intruder in her kitchen, but this time she would imagine herself being unafraid. If she is successful with this a few times over the next couple of days, the feeling and even the memory of her fear from the incident, should subside.

A final method of using visualisation is during what is called 'systematic desensitisation'. This is when your clients are asked to continually visualise the fearful scene over and over again but each time try to consciously relax during the visualisation, either by using the deep muscle relaxation or the relaxation meditation. For this exercise they also need to rate how strong the feeling is, and to keep visualising until it is lessened. This type of visualisation is a bit more stressful than the others and you will have to watch your clients' body-language carefully so as not to re-truamatise them, but it has been used with success.

BODY BIOFEEDBACK

Another modern trauma technique is to use feedback from the body itself.

Feedback on the client's level of anxiety

For this technique your client must give you ongoing feedback as to the anxiety (tension) they are feeling in their bodies, also rated on a scale of one to ten.

Let us again use the case study of Peter:

Counsellor: *'Peter, on a scale of one to ten, how would you rate your anxiety at this moment?'*

Peter: *'I would say an eight'*

Counsellor: *'All right. So we know you can handle an eight, but if you feel it going up to nine or ten please let me know and we will take a break'*

This exercise will serve two purposes. First it will give Peter a sense of control over the counselling and second, it will allow the coun-sellor to keep an eye on Peters' bodily tension and anxiety levels and to know what areas Peter finds most stressful, that is, when he reports these levels rising. The idea is to focus on these areas using empowerment skills until Peter reports a large drop in his bodily tension and anxiety levels.

Visualisation and acupressure

This particular exercise uses visualisation and acupressure together with body biofeedback. However, for this you will need a specialised knowledge of acupressure points. If you do not have this training, it is best that you refer your clients to a trained acupressure specialist, or get one to assist you during the counselling.

The idea is to ask your client to recall (visualise) those scenes that are particularly stressful, and as they report feeling fearful or anxious, you tap or press continuously on their acupressure points. They should tell you when your pressing or tapping on a particular point has a positive effect, and as you continue, they must once again rate (on a scale of one to ten) how their fear or anxiety has been lessened.

Body Tremors (TRE)

Once again, this is a way of empowering traumatised clients that needs special training. It is called TRE and consists of six exercises designed to bring on natural tremors in the body in a controlled and sustained way. This process is said to release the deep muscular tension from trauma held in the body.

When the tremors are evoked, they travel along the spine to the whole body. The body responds to this as a signal that the trauma is past, releasing the tension which accompanies the negative feelings and bringing itself back into balance. Once again, if you are not trained in this modality it is best to refer your client to a qualified practitioner, or have one help you during the early sessions of your counselling.

More details on these biofeedback exercises fall outside the scope of this guide. If you wish to use them during your trauma counselling it will be best to do a course with a registered trainer.

ANALYSING, LINKING AND SUMMARISING SKILLS

In the later stages of the process you will be able to use rational thinking skills to analyse, link and summarise what your client has told you and use this information for empowerment and mastery.

Analysing, linking and summarising skills are usually more successful after you've explored your clients' feelings and they are in a better place emotionally, as they will need to think more clearly, rationally and logically. Sometimes, due to the powerful emotions, their perceptions and thinking are not reasonable but rather negative and self-recriminating.

This means that you will have to apply your mind to remember key facts and issues, such as your clients' perceptions of the incident and the reasonableness of their self-talk. There may also be deep-seated concerns that they have not mentioned, such as possible pregnancy in the case of rape. You can carefully raise these concerns if you are able to infer them from their verbal or non-verbal cues, or simply by '*listening between the lines*', but it is not a good idea to introduce issues which are not actually there, such as guilt or self-blame.

ANALYSING SKILLS

During the later stages you will be using more of your reasoning and analysing abilities, especially during the stage of empowerment (stage four). This most apparent during *cognitive restructuring,* when you measure your clients' self-talk, beliefs and perceptions against what is reasonable, objective, rational and true. Earlier on you were urged to remember their thoughts and perceptions and during the empowerment stage you will try to correct any thoughts which are negative and not reasonable and only adding to your clients' unpleasant emotions.

You may also find yourself using logical thinking to point out any inconsistencies in the account of the incident provided by your clients, but remember that your aim should be to counter negativity and empower your client and certainly not to embarrass or criticise them in any way.

During the mastery stage, you also need to analyse the information given earlier by your clients to assist them to come up with real-istic options to help them reduce their stress and return a sense of control and normality to their lives. You also need to highlight any outstanding issues or areas of concern that will need more attention, such as family, medical or legal problems.

These will all form part of a plan to achieve mastery over their sit-uation. However, remember to stay within their frame of reference and possibilities, taking into consideration their education level, real-life home and work situations, financial means and coping mechanisms. These are all factors which you will have to consider when collaborating with your clients to compile the plan.

LINKING SKILLS

Often, when you begin to unpack, analyse and link up the informa-tion given to you by your clients, you begin to see underlying issues, themes or trends. They may have had a difficult childhood or a past which has left them with low self-esteem or even depression, and this now causes them to blame themselves for no good reason.

It may also be the case that they were not really dealing well with life before the incident, not being a coping person, and this is now affecting their present trauma. Any stress in their present lives or their past which has not been properly dealt with will only make things worse. Trauma can also be complicated by grieving, such as in the case of a violent death of a close family member.

Look for hidden associations and try to *link* what happened in the past to the present. In this way you will have more insight into their situation, their thoughts and feelings and be able to make use of this information during the empowerment stage.

SUMMARISING SKILLS

This skill is used together with linking to critically look at your clients' self-talk and perceptions of the incident with the view of challenging them. The powerful negative emotions involved in trauma can cause very harmful self-talk which can emotionally cripple your clients, and the idea of summarising and using information given to you earlier is to counter these negative thoughts and beliefs of self-blame and regret, move your clients out of the cycle of helplessness and give them back a sense of control. This is normally done during the empowerment stage.

Let us use Sandra's case study of her being robbed in her car at an intersection:

Counsellor: *'You told me earlier that he had a gun pointed at you and this forced you to give him your bag. It seems to me that you may be blaming yourself for things that were out of your control'*

Counsellor: *'Let's take another look at what you did during this incident...'*

The counsellor will gather and summarise information she gave him earlier to show Sandra that her perception of the situation was skewed by her fear and that she actually acted correctly in spite of being terrified'

Counsellor: '*From this it seems that you actually did very well to get through this situation*'

Summarising skills can also be used at the end of the counselling process during the stage of mastery to give an overview of what has been achieved and to congratulate your client.

To conclude the case study:

Counsellor: *'We have looked at your actions during the incident and you agreed that there was not much else that you could have done. In hindsight, you have actually done very well. ' You got him away from you very quickly before he was able to hurt you.'*

Sandra: *'Yes, I suppose you are right'.*

SKILLS TO HELP YOUR CLIENTS RETURN TO MASTERY

Mastery means that, after a period of healing, your clients' lives have (more or less) returned to normal. This may take a few months and it is for this reason that proper trauma counselling cannot be done in one or two sessions. There are a number of skills that you can use to help your clients at this time, but remember that this only happens at the end of the empowerment stage when their emotions and negative self-talk have been addressed and they are able to make good decisions.

Looking at their options and putting together a plan

Your clients need to be guided through a process of looking at viable options which will (hopefully) return their lives to normal. This should include their needs for ongoing support, medical treatment and security and putting together a plan of action to address these needs. Note that this usually takes place during the final phase of *re-organisation* and *reintegration*.

Your aim at this time should be to help your clients come up with ideas to deal with outstanding needs or issues and compile action steps for each issue to return their lives to relative normality. Once again, the final choice of action-steps should be left to the clients, as this is important for self-discovery and they need to take ownership and responsibility for the plan. In other words, don't simply give your clients your own ready-made solutions. If they are struggling to come up with ideas, you can offer suggestions, but they must make the decision to include it in their plan.

With the skill of option-handling you will need to be able to first clarify the outstanding issues and then use linking, summarising and analysing skills working in collaboration with your clients. Discuss what they think they will need to put their lives back on track and resolve any important problems still facing them such as medical and legal issues, personal and home security and practical support, anything that could stop them from returning to mastery.

Remember to keep in mind your clients' real-life situation, such as their finances, home and work situations, family setups and coping abilities, as well as their *frame of reference*, which contains their backgrounds, cultures and customs, attitudes and beliefs, standards and values. These are all factors you need to consider when helping them to draw up their plans for mastery.

Helping them let go of old defence mechanisms

Many traumatised persons withdraw into themselves and start to avoid people and places. In the beginning this is fine as it gives them the time and space to reflect and heal. However, if it carries on for a long time, they will find themselves running out of support. Support and encouragement from family and friends must not be underestimated, and it is actually necessary to re-integrate with one's family and social circle in order to achieve mastery of the situation. You may remember that the final phase of the trauma process is quite aptly named *re-organisation* and *re-integration*. You may need to assist your clients to restore family communication and social contact if this has become a problem.

Case study

You will remember the case study of Janet who was threatened in her kitchen by a knife-wielding intruder and robbed of her handbag. Let us see how this has affected her life.

Janet is now fearful most of the time and does not go out anymore. She has become negative and withdrawn and has stopped her normal family and social activities. After a few months her family and friends have stopped coming around and she find herself in a position where she can no longer count on their support. It is unfortunate, but this can often happen. Immediately after the incident (impact phase) everyone rallies around, but this can change as soon as the client enters the recoil phase without having had counselling and tends to become negative, irritable and withdrawn.

When looking at Janet's situation you would try to help her rebuild her relationships and find options that would help her get support in the short, medium and long-term. In this regard she could return to steps that she took in the past to keep family contact, *present* coping mechanisms as well as future possibilities that are open to her (past, present and future options).

Past:

Counsellor: '*How often did you see your family in the past?*'

Janet: '*I used to visit my brother every week before the incident and phone my family at least once a week*'.

Counsellor: '*And your friends?*'

Janet: '*I was also very busy before the incident. I had a number of close friends and used to go to church and social functions regularly. I was also active on social media*'

As part of her plan for mastery Janet would need to be encouraged to continue with these earlier activities, especially reaching out to family and friends for support.

Counsellor: '*Do you think you could start up some of these activities again? They seemed to work for you in the past.*'

Janet: '*I suppose I could.*' '*I really do want to see my family and friends again*'

Practical support

Janet may also need help with daily tasks. In this case you would assist her to look at her present situation and coping mechanisms.

Present:

Counsellor: '*How do you presently fetch the children from school?*'

Janet: '*I contact my sister if I need help with the children*'

Counsellor: '*I assume that you will continue to do this until things have gone back to normal?*'

Janet: '*Yes, my sister has agreed to go on with this arrangement*'

If Janet is not able to offer any present solutions for the normalisation of her day-to-day routine, you could introduce and discuss possible future coping strategies.

Future:

Counsellor: '*What do you think you can do in the future to make things easier for you?*'

Janet: '*I would like it if I could be given a different position at work. My present job does not allow me much time for myself and my children.*'

Counsellor: '*Is that a possibility?*'

Janet: '*Yes, I do plan to talk to my supervisor about it*'

If, during this planning process Janet is not able to come up with any suitable ideas and options herself, you can assist by offering suggestions, but it is important that she make the decision to include them in her plan. She will also need to take responsibility for, and ownership of the plan, and be motivated enough to carry it out.

Every idea she includes in her plan should be measured against a number of criteria: For instance, Is it useful? Is it practical? And is it achievable? Those options that she selects must be broken down further into action-steps and linked together to form her plan for mastery.

PUTTING TOGETHER A PLAN FOR MASTERY

Having a plan helps to lessen feelings of helplessness and will give your clients a purpose and direction as well as control over their lives. An ideal outcome for mastery would therefore be that your clients are able to successfully implement their plan containing practical steps to reorganise their lives and to deal with the long-term effects of the trauma they have experienced.

The plan must include steps to assist them to re-engage with their home, work, friends and family and ultimately to put together the shattered pieces of their psyche. This means helping them rebuild their self-esteem and self-confidence and regain the sense of being in control of their lives.

As shown, putting together the plan is a collaborative process in which both the clients and the counsellor are involved. The steps you agree upon must take your clients' frame of reference and real-life situations into account and must not be too complicated. It could begin with a series of baby steps and be later changed if need be. It can also include short, medium and long term goals and objectives. Changes can be made later during follow-up sessions when your clients report back on the success or failure of their action-steps.

Let us now have a look at a number of examples of action-steps using Janet's case study.

Janet's concerns about home and personal security

A short-term option to allay Janet's fears could include moving in with her relatives or friends until her insecurities subside. The problem is that she has her children staying with her. This will make moving out difficult.

Another short-term possibility could be to upgrade her security system at home by fitting security gates and intercom access control. She already has a panic button system with armed response, but as she was surprised in her kitchen, she never had time to use it. .

If her stressfulness continues, a medium-term option may be moving to a more secure residential area or housing complex, but this will depend on her money situation, her travelling distance to work, if she has pets, as well as other factors. These are all things that will have to be considered. Other less costly options could be joining the neighbourhood watch or a social network dedicated to reporting on crime.

The problem is that even with the most advanced security systems, peoples' personal safety can't always be fully guaranteed. The idea is to improve her feelings of security and hopefully over time, her fears will eventually subside.

Janet's concerns about her ongoing anxiety

If the practical measures she takes do not help to reduce her anxiety within a few weeks, Janet will need to be referred to a psychologist or psychiatrist for long-term therapy. There may be deep-seated factors hindering her recovery, even the possibility of disorders or P.T.S.D.

Referrals to other professionals should also form part of her plan.

Janet's medical problems

The stress associated with trauma can set off any prior medical conditions. For instance, before the incident Janet had high blood pressure. This has now been worsened by what happened. If it does not get better soon she will have to return to the doctor for extra medication.

Janet's legal issues

It is also possible that the intruder is caught and Janet may have to attend court to give evidence. In other cases involving legal processes, they can also be very expensive. Janet's plan may need to include referral to a lawyer to help her deal with any legal issues.

DEALING WITH THEIR OTHER OBSTACLES TO MASTERY

During the option-handling and planning stages you would also have to look at how your clients are coping with other issues or challenges in re-organising and reintegrating their lives. For example, your clients may be battling with other concerns such as financial problems and family or partner relationships. As before, collaborate with your clients to agree on action-steps to deal with these issues, such as debt-coaching or longer-term counselling to help manage these situations.

There are also a number of other methods you can use to support your clients' journey to mastery.

Teaching your clients coping skills

If it is clear to you that your clients do not have the necessary coping skills to achieve mastery, there are ways of improving the situation. For example, you could encourage them to do personal growth or skills-development courses or to use the services of a life-coach for long-term training in self-empowerment. If you have the knowledge there is nothing wrong with you yourself teaching your clients new coping skills during later counselling sessions, such as using positive affirmations and meditation.

In the case of health issues, they could consider training in yoga, tai chi and body-talk with suitably qualified practitioners. These will also help to improve their states of mind and emotional wellness.

Helping your clients with personal growth and development

When working with self-mastery you should also be prepared to guide your clients to explore themselves on a deeper level during which time they can discover new strengths and capacities to improve their feelings of competency and control. This will assist them to be better equipped to handle future challenges in their lives. In fact, the desired outcome of the whole process of trauma counselling is to help your clients return to normal and to build *resilience.*

For example, you can improve their motivation by redirecting their thoughts to a project or idea which excites and enthuses them, keeps them busy and productive and boosts their self-esteem. One such idea is writing (and becoming a published writer). Keeping a journal and creative writing is quite effective in helping trauma-tised persons express their thoughts and feelings. It is also, in itself, therapeutic. Art or writing can also be empowering by helping your clients discover meaning and direction in their lives. I have found that this works especially well with depressed clients.

Another path of personal growth involves helping others by joining an organisation for the less fortunate. Once focus is taken off the self, people tend to discover a higher meaning and purpose.

A final word on mastery

Self-empowerment is very important for mastery. If you are successful, you could help your clients improve their emotional wellness, resilience and coping skills. In fact these are the ideal outcomes for the final phase of *reorganisation and reintegration*. Stress and challenges will always be there, simply due to the normal home and work crises that occur in the life of any person.

In order to build this resilience and a sense of personal responsibility, you should not be pressured into doing anything which your clients are capable of doing for themselves, such as making contact with family or friends, setting up appointments with doctors or lawyers, or arranging for work to be done at home. If your clients are empowered to accept personal responsibility they are more likely to cope the next time they encounter a crisis.

CHAPTER FIVE

A DIAGRAM OF A TRAUMA COUNSELLING PROCESS

This is a diagram of a suggested, structured, outcomes-based trauma counselling process of five stages which highlights the different skills needed at each stage. Stages one to three would be suitable for the impact and recoil phases, and stages four and five for the third and final phase of re-organisation and re-integration.

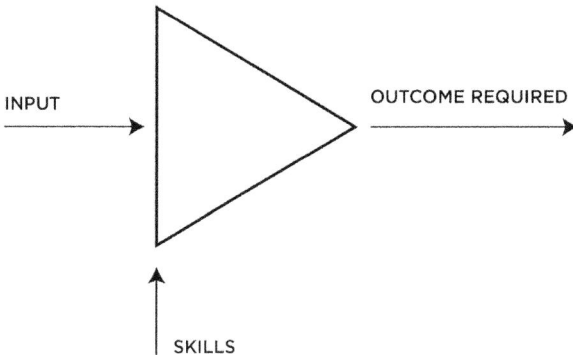

INPUT →

OUTCOME REQUIRED →

↑
SKILLS

STAGES OF THE TRAUMA COUNSELLING PROCESS

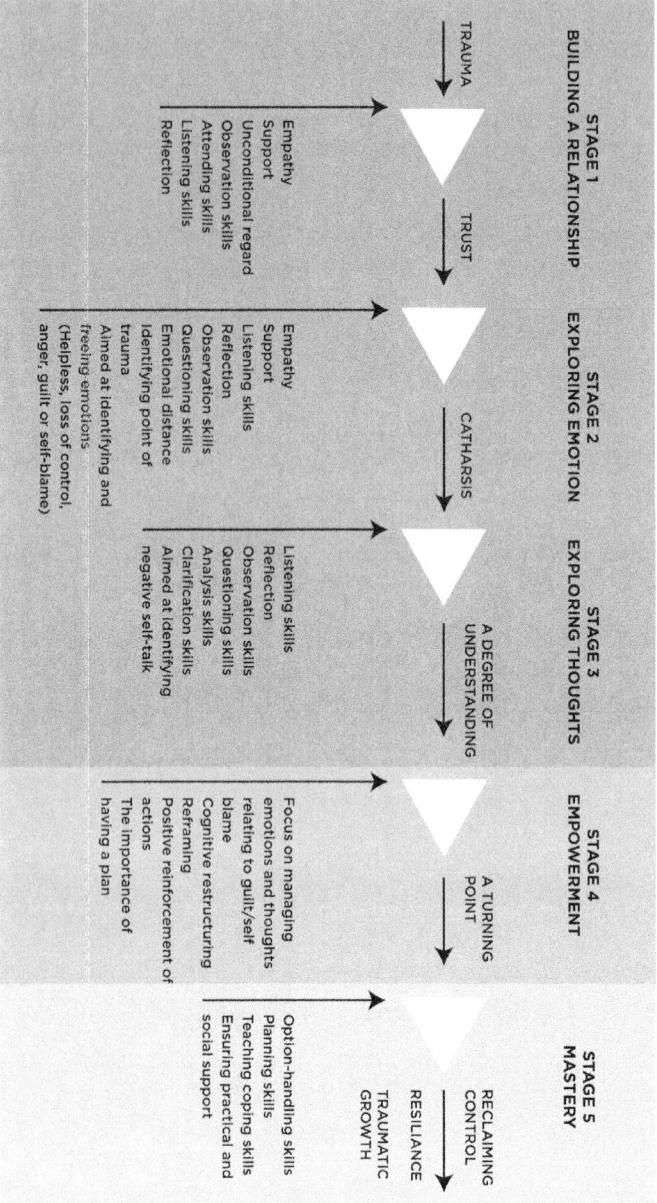

STAGE 1 BUILDING A RELATIONSHIP	STAGE 2 EXPLORING EMOTION	STAGE 3 EXPLORING THOUGHTS	STAGE 4 EMPOWERMENT	STAGE 5 MASTERY
TRAUMA → TRUST	TRUST → CATHARSIS	CATHARSIS → A DEGREE OF UNDERSTANDING	A DEGREE OF UNDERSTANDING → A TURNING POINT	A TURNING POINT → RECLAIMING CONTROL → RESILIANCE → TRAUMATIC GROWTH
Empathy Support Unconditional regard Observation skills Attending skills Listening skills Reflection	Empathy Support Listening skills Reflection Observation skills Questioning skills Emotional distance Identifying point of trauma Aimed at identifying and freeing emotions (Helpless, loss of control, anger, guilt or self-blame)	Listening skills Reflection Observation skills Questioning skills Analysis skills Clarification skills Aimed at identifying negative self-talk	Focus on managing emotions and thoughts relating to guilt/self blame Cognitive restructuring Reframing Positive reinforcement of actions The importance of having a plan	Option-handling skills Planning skills Teaching coping skills Ensuring practical and social support

A FEW GUIDELINES FOR THE PROCESS

In order to point out the important processes and skills needed for trauma counselling I have divided the trauma counselling process into a number of stages. You will see that for each stage you will need a number of specific skills and each stage also has an ideal outcome. Ideally you should not move on to the next stage until you have achieved the outcome of the previous stage.

I have also spoken earlier about how the trauma responses unfold over a number of weeks, and, as a result, it is not advisable to try to finish all these different stages in one counselling session.

However, this does depend on where your clients find themselves in the trauma process when they come in for counselling. In other words, if they are not in the impact or acute phase, or have already had professional treatment, or the incident is long past, you may be able to finish all the stages in one session.

A safe guideline is also to stay with the earlier stages until you are sure that your clients are ready to move onto the later stages. Obviously, you must plan for the worst-case scenario, which would be a situation in which your client has just been through a traumatic incident and is in the '*impact*' or *acute phase* of the process.

It can also happen that you believe that you have dealt with your clients' feelings and self-talk but during a later session the disturbing images, crippling emotions and recriminating thoughts return. This means that you have to go back to the earlier stages until they have been fully dealt with. However, if, after the first session you find that your client is not responding to counselling at all, it is possible that the trauma has already become a disorder and it would be best to refer them to a professional for medical care. Lay counsellors are not qualified to deal with mental disorders.

Let us now work through the different stages:

STAGE 1: BUILDING A GOOD RELA-TIONSHIP WITH YOUR CLIENTS

This stage begins the moment your clients enter the counselling room and you engage with them. The goal here is to present a favourable first impression, quickly establish rapport and finally, build the important relationship of trust which will allow you to gain their cooperation for the process to follow.

Observing what is happening

Use your observation skills immediately to read your clients' body language, gauge their emotional state and see which phase of the trauma process they are in. For instance, clients in the impact phase will be highly distressed and you may have to help them to their seats, while those in the recoil phase will possibly be less willing to be counselled. These clients are often brought for counselling by family or friends who can see that they are actually not coping, although they may not admit it. They will appear normal at first but as soon as you hit a nerve you will see emotions coming out. Finally, clients in the re-organisation and integration phase will act quite matter of fact, and their past trauma will only become evident if you open up old 'wounds'. What these clients normally need is affirmation, encouragement and help with some practical issues.

Giving physical support

Badly-traumatised clients in the impact phase may be quite help-less and you may need to actually take them by the arm and lead them to a suitable seating position. Others in the later *recoil* or *reorganisation* and *reintegration* phases shouldn't require this kind of support, unless they have had some sort of a relapse.

Attending properly to your clients

Attending in this case means being fully aware of what is happening and responding immediately to your clients' needs for physical, emotional and psychological support. Your initial approach should be one of empathy, unconditional acceptance and unconditional positive regard as shown in your attitude, body-language, voice and choice of words. When first introducing yourself, use your first name. You do not want to appear distant and it also helps to place your clients at ease. For instance, 'I'm John. I am a trauma counsellor and I'm here to help you.' You may have to introduce yourself each time during later sessions, as clients in the *impact phase* may be so traumatised that they do not remember your name at first.

Trying to identify with them and match their language skills

Try to identify with your clients and match their language and level of education. In other words, do not use fancy terms they will not be able to understand. If your client does not speak English, try to find a family member to be an interpreter, or else let a counsellor who is fluent in their language take over the counselling. If a client does not speak or understand English, this should be known beforehand and an interpreter arranged before the session. It doesn't help rushing around at the last moment looking for an interpreter or struggling on with a session when neither you nor your client actually understands what is going on.

Your mood should also closely follow that of your clients. For instance, if their mood is depressed, do not talk to them in a frivolous or joking manner. Respect their pain. Later on, when you are busy with empowerment, you can try to lift their mood with a more light-hearted approach.

Listening and reflecting

Do not 'dive into' the deeper counselling processes. First put your clients at ease using *small talk*, listening, reflection and simple questioning.

The case study of Cathy:

Counsellor: *'I understand that you are married and have three children?'*

Cathy: *'Yes, I have three wonderful children'*

Counsellor: *'That's great, and I trust they are all well?'*

Cathy: '*Yes, thank you*'

If your client is badly traumatised, in the impact phase and in distress, small talk might not help. The best would be to immediately respond with attention, empathy, comforting and assurances. In fact, it is a good idea if you are briefed by someone on your clients' situation before you begin, as well as on the circumstances of the incident, so that are prepared and do not walk blindly into a desperate situation.

Reassuring your clients

Once your clients are composed, reassure them that you will be with them every step of the way and tell them briefly about the process you will be following. Clients in the impact phase often feel helpless. Knowing beforehand that they will be treated with care and not re-traumatised will help to lower their anxiety and give them a feeling of control over what happens during the session. They should also be assured of the total confidentiality of the session.

Helping them relax

If they are very distressed, try some deep breathing and relaxation techniques to help them relax. You could also use meditation, visualisation, body-biofeedback techniques or by inducing tremors if you have skill in these areas. These are discussed under the section of empowerment skills.

'Normalising' their symptoms

Traumatised persons go through a wide range of emotional, psychological and physical responses immediately after the incident and have a number of unpleasant symptoms. They often think there is something horribly wrong with them because they are feeling this way and this only makes the stress worse. 'Normalising' in this case means assuring them that their unpleasant feelings, negative thoughts and images and bodily symptoms are normal for what they have been through. In fact, they are to be expected. This should lower their anxiety somewhat and stop them thinking that their lives are spiralling out of control.

Cementing your relationship

These few steps can be considered the most important part of stage one and will hopefully cement a relationship of trust. This relationship now becomes a '*safe space*' for your clients to share their emotions and thoughts freely and openly and it is now likely that they would be willing to return for the following sessions.

In some cases, caring and giving physical and empathetic support may take up the whole first session, and you may not even get to stage two and three to explore their feelings and thoughts in more depth. That is fine. The whole idea of the first session is to reach out to your clients, build a relationship for later sessions and normalise and hopefully soothe their out-of-control feelings and negative thoughts. The first session also gives them hope by their knowing that someone is there to help them, as well as strength to get through the night and to cope until the next session, which should be the following day.

Giving practical guidance until the next session

At the end of the first session offer your clients some practical steps to tide them over until you see them again. With regard to their emotional distress and symptoms, try to discourage them from using strong medication or drinking excessively to block out the pain. This will only give them temporary relief, but will mask the trauma and delay their moving through the trauma process. Their minds and emotions need to adjust to what has taken place and this will not happen if their feelings and thoughts are blotted out by alcohol or strong medication. Tablets for headaches, stomach pains, diarrhoea and insomnia are fine, as well as the occasional glass of wine or spirits.

Also encourage them not to take long sick leave with the idea of recovering at home. This usually does not happen and they often end up languishing alone at home by themselves. They will need company and support, and if family or friends cannot spend a few days with them, it would be better if they soon go back to work, as their work colleagues and managers are usually supportive, especially if the company has an *employee assistance programme*. They can always ask to be given light office duties if they do not feel up to their usual demanding job. It is crucial for them not to be alone.

Praising and supporting them

Also praise them for their courage in being prepared to come for counselling and to share the details of the incident with you. It is difficult to have to share your pain and feelings with others.

STAGE 2: EXPLORING YOUR CLIENTS' FEELINGS AND EMOTIONS

By now you should be able to see the connection between emotions, thoughts and behaviour in trauma, especially how ongoing negative thinking can give rise to and prolong intense feelings of fear, helplessness, guilt, self-blame and the feeling of having lost control over one's life.

In this stage (Stage two) we first tackle the intense feelings and emotions which are crippling your clients. The reason for this is that their negative thoughts need to still be identified, but in order to do this, they have to be able to think clearly and this is not always possible when they are under the spell of powerful emotions.

Using your relationship to explore their feelings

During stage one you were able to build a relationship with your clients. You used simple listening skills to reflect and show your concern, empathy and support. This continues in stage two, but now you add a new phase, the deeper exploration of their emotions. Once again, this has to be done in a totally non-judgemental manner, with an even greater focus on empathy, responsiveness and unconditional positive regard, as, once you open up their feelings, your clients are very vulnerable and will most likely need more support.

Not letting them relive the experience

In stage two you will need to use *emotional distance*, the skill I discussed earlier. This also helps you to gauge if your clients are strong enough to begin sharing their painful emotions. Remember that if your clients are in the later phases of the trauma process and are already coping well, you probably will not need to use any emotional distance.

At this time you will need to use special skills to make sure that your clients are not re-traumatised. The last thing you want is for them to relive the experience. This will undo all the good work you have done during stage one. Tell them that the incident is over and you don't want them to go back and re-experience it, just to tell you what they remember in the form of a narrative.

Your main approach at this stage should be to prime your clients for the difficult questioning to come and to get their permission to expose their innermost feelings.

Use Janet's case study as an example:

Counsellor: *'Janet, do you think you are ready to talk to me about the incident?'*

Janet: *'I don't know. I feel very scared'*

Counsellor: *'I do understand that this is difficult, but it is the best way of helping you'*

'Would it be in order if I ask you a few questions on your feelings at the moment?'

Your considerate requests at this time should provide your clients with the feeling that they have some control over what is happening during the counselling and this can reduce their anxiety and feelings of helplessness.

Important note

In practice, this stage (stage two, that of exploring emotions) cannot actually be seen as separate from stage three (that of exploring thoughts), as your clients' feelings and thoughts will usually just emerge spontaneously and intermingle as they tell you their story. What I mean to say is that you cannot tell your clients to hold back their thinking and focus only on their emotions. You have to try to bring this about by the way you phrase your questions. If they do express their thoughts and self-talk at the same time as their feelings, it is up to you to sort them out.

In other words, stage two and three actually flow back and forth into one another and are merely shown separately in order to show the different approaches and skills involved for each stage. The onus is therefore on you to respond to both emotions and thoughts at appropriate times.

The 'short version'

If you decide that it is necessary for you to use emotional distance, ask them first to give you a *short factual version* of the incident, without the feelings and emotions (if that is at all possible). This becomes a less-threatening warm-up for the deeper processes, a brief outline of the facts of the incident. You are gradually intro-ducing your clients to the intense emotional narrative to come. This will lower your clients' feelings of helplessness and loss of control and allow you to see their emotional and mental capacity before you begin with in-depth exploration.

Note

If your clients are in the later recovery stages you will not have to be so careful. You can begin by asking for the full sequence of events, together with their feelings and thoughts every step of the way.

Listening and reflecting

The basic approach you will use during stage two is that of listening skills such as feedback and reflection to encourage your clients to share their emotions deeply. Listening includes the skilled use of silence to bring on these feelings, as this is what you want. In other words, the aim of stage two is for you to help your clients to feel, to acknowledge and to describe every emotion or feeling which they have, and to encourage *catharsis*, when they start letting go of the tension from these emotions in the form of tremors, shivering, sobbing and tears. This is in itself, therapeutic, and when you as the counsellor acknowledge and encourage these actions and feelings, the effect is so much greater.

When you believe your clients are ready, ask them to share their narrative in detail. Your job is to reflect, clarify, identify and acknowledge each emotion as it emerges.

The most likely emotions of clients in the impact or acute phase will be fear, helplessness and the feeling of totally losing control. At the same time they are likely to be recalling vivid images of the event which are setting off these emotions and may need a lot of physical support. Clients in the later stages may also speak of feelings of guilt or self-blame.

If you are a female counsellor it is fine to hug or hold your clients. However, if you are a male with a female client, I would suggest being more careful and possibly just placing your hand on their shoulders. Watch out for a reaction, and if she pulls away, this means she does not want to be touched.

If they break down and begin crying at any time, reflect, encourage and acknowledge this. But if they begin to lose control, it means that they have gone too deeply into the experience and you will need to try other distancing skills such as the third-person perspective to pull them out and keep them from re-living the experience. If you wish, you can also try deep breathing, relaxation, meditation and visualisation techniques to help them relax.

Emotional distance also protects you as the counsellor. If you get pulled into the pit of despair in which your clients find themselves you will not be able to continue. This is called *vicarious trauma* and usually affects those who work frequently with victims of trauma. Especially in stage two you need to guard against being caught up in your clients' emotions by keeping an emotional distance while still being empathetic.

Beginning to question for emotions, but paying attention to sudden changes

During stage two you can begin with a few questions about their present feelings, but be extra careful to note any sudden changes to their emotional and mental states. If you are counselling online or over the phone pay particular attention to listening for emotion in their voices.

As they narrate the events of the incident, they could become very distressed and may need extra support. This means keeping a close eye on changes in their body-language, facial expressions and voices. You will see a strong emotion or a moment of distress by a sudden shift to a defensive body posture, such as their falling forward to close up their bodies, or quickly folding their arms and becoming quiet. This will either be in response to something you have asked or said which has hit a nerve, or else a sudden thought or image which evokes a strong emotion. If this happens you should immediately stop your questioning, move closer and lean forward towards them to offer physical support.

Once they have composed themselves, again ask their permission and prime them for the next question before you carry on.

Let us again return to Janet's case study

Counsellor: '*I am sorry if I upset you. Unfortunately this is the only way I can help you.*'

Janet: '*I know*' '*It is just very upsetting.*'

Counsellor: '*I understand.*' *Are you ready to continue telling me what happened?*'

As before, if your clients are in distress, they need to be primed for the next question. If a question is particularly sensitive, it is always best to warn them of this beforehand.

As your clients continue with their narrative, listen attentively and combine listening and reflection with questioning. Your aim is to identify and discuss any troubling images, feelings or emotions, whilst at the same time giving your client plenty of empathy and support. They will probably also have negative thoughts at the same time, but for this stage, try to focus on their emotions.

Identifying the moment of trauma

One of the most important tasks of stage two is to uncover the *point or moment of trauma*. This will be a vivid, frightening image or a powerful thought or emotion which sets off the trauma response. This usually happens in the instant when the clients are abruptly and frighteningly made aware of the reality of the situation or the threat of death. For instance, the sight of a gun or knife pointed at them, or the terrifying view of a dead spouse or partner.

We can imagine the emotions associated with such an experience, shock, horror, or terror, which are typical of trauma, and thoughts such as '*I am going to die*' in the case of a threat of a weapon, or in the case of the deceased family member; '*He/she is gone*', '*I am alone*'. Even the sight or smell of blood, being grabbed by the perpetrator, or threats such as '*I am going to kill you*', can bring about the moment of trauma and feelings of total helplessness.

These vivid images and sense-experiences at the moment of trauma will repeatedly keep coming back as flashbacks or thoughts which can totally take over the clients' normal daily life and routine.

Once you have identified this moment of trauma it becomes a good place to begin exploring your clients' feelings and emotions as well as the thoughts and self-beliefs which arose at that crucial time. Once you begin questioning, watch your clients' reactions carefully to ensure they are not reliving the incident. In stage two you are looking for 'happenings' and the feelings which arose from each of these experiences, so use open-ended questions and cue words to identify those painful areas which will need special attention.

Here are a few examples of open-ended questions with the cue words; what, see (saw), hear (heard) and feel.

Counsellor: '*Can you tell me what happened*'

Counsellor: '*What was it that he said?*' (Here you are trying to establish the facts)

Counsellor: '*Can you tell me what you saw at that moment?*' (Here you are looking for the vivid images which are filling your clients' mind)

Counsellor: '*What do you remember when the gun was fired?*' (Here you are looking for other memories that could be causing them distress)

Counsellor: '*What did you feel at the time?*' (Remember that you are trying to identify your client's feelings and emotions every step of the way)

Be guided by your clients' answers during this in-depth exploration. Listen and respond to each reply with empathy and encourage them to release the pain and trauma as you discuss each area.

Ideally, during this stage you are trying to bring about *catharsis* to release their stress. This usually happens when they begin to shiver, shake, cry or sob and you can visibly see the tension leaving their bodies. You can actually encourage these actions to help them release this tension.

STAGE 3: EXPLORING YOUR CLIENTS' THINKING

If stage two was successful, your clients should appear a little more composed and you can begin with more difficult questioning in stage three. You are now trying to get through to the underlying self-talk that is leading to their tension and stress. When you see that they are more relaxed, ask them if they are ready to go through some of the details again, but this time focus on their thinking and beliefs about the incident. Explain to them that this is, unfortunately, also necessary for their recovery.

Carrying on observing

Your clients may become emotional again in stage three during reflection and questioning as you will be asking them to recall the fearful thoughts that entered their minds during the incident. You will need to watch their reactions closely for any sudden changes in body language which will show that they are in distress and you should stop and offer immediate support if this happens. Once again, if you are counselling online or over the phone, focus on changes in their voices.

Listening and questioning

Once again, use your listening and questioning skills to encourage your clients to return to the negative thoughts and beliefs which started with the *moment of trauma* and are still present in their self-talk. As before, prepare your clients for any difficult questions and keep emotional distance in mind if they become very emotional or are in distress. Once again use open-ended questions and cue words to identify any negative self-talk and self-recriminating beliefs which are at the core of their emotions. Many of these thoughts and beliefs will not be rational, being formed at a time when they were very emotional and not thinking clearly.

Let us again use the case study of Peter

Counsellor: *'What went through your mind at that moment?'*

Peter: *'That I should be standing up to this person.'*

Counsellor: *'You believed you should do something?'*

Peter: *'Yes, A man should be able to look after himself'*

(Notice the myth that men must be competent and capable in everything they do)

Counsellor: *'What are you telling yourself now?'*

Peter: '*That I am a failure as a man and that no-one will respect me'*

Peter's belief that he is a failure has taken over his thinking and is making him feel ashamed and depressed. This is on top of the stress he has from been threatened with death by the hijacker. This is an example of the type of thoughts associated with guilt or self-blame, and you would have to isolate, identify and challenge this self-talk in the empowerment stage.

Making sure (clarifying)

Certain thoughts and beliefs are linked to specific emotions. For instance, 'I am going to die' (fear); 'I will never see him/her again' (loss); 'If only I had not gone that route' (regret) or 'I should have acted differently' (self-blame). As seen in the previous case study, beliefs which may, or may not be true can also lead to powerful emotions, such as 'It was my fault' (guilt or self-blame) or 'I'm a failure' (feelings of despair).

If you are not sure about the content of the self-talk driving your clients' emotions, keep reflecting, questioning and clarifying until you have identified all their thoughts. If you are doing counselling over the phone you can write them down. If you are doing face-to face counselling rather try to remember them as you do not want to distract your clients by writing while you are counselling.

You need to know exactly what these thoughts are for the next stage of empowerment. This means exploring deeply and getting to the core beliefs in their thinking and self-talk. What you are trying to achieve in stage three is to identify and fully unpack your client's negative thoughts, beliefs and self-talk resulting from the traumatic incident. You will probably be jumping between stage two and stage three, as exploring these thoughts will most likely result in emotional responses which you will also need to manage.

Session one should not go past this stage (stage three). This will give your clients time to adjust to the counselling process which is also very stressful for them.

Arranging for more sessions

A person with severe trauma cannot be counselled properly in only one session and certainly not online or over the phone. More coun-selling sessions should be arranged. In the case of recent trauma and your clients were in the impact phase, make arrangements with their family or friends for them to be brought in for the second session the next day. If it is past trauma and the client is coping well, a week later would be fine.

If you are counselling traumatised staff at company premises, the additional sessions need to be arranged with the manager or company representative. Your clients simply cannot be left to their own devices after only one session. In this case you should inform them that arrangements have been made with their managers. This will take the pressure off them. Knowing that they are not alone and you are with them for all the way will also reassure your clients.

STAGE 4: EMPOWERING YOUR CLIENTS TO COPE

This is probably the most important stage of trauma counselling. At this point you have to start using thinking strategies to help your clients let go of negative thoughts and irrational beliefs and to start seeing their role in the incident in a more positive light. If their thinking and actions can be empowered, they will begin to let go of, or at least be able to manage, the crippling emotions such as fear, helplessness and guilt that have led to the feeling of having lost control of their lives.

Analysing the situation carefully

This stage is different from the others as the focus is more on you applying your mind to analyse your clients' thoughts and actions during the incident, which are contained in the negative self-talk and beliefs which you identified in stage three.

The aim of this stage is to try and remove this negative thinking, doubt, self-blame and fear from their minds by showing them that much of which they believe or fear is not real, not reasonable, not rational or simply not true, and that there are a number of other ways in which the incident can be seen.

By now you should know all the facts of the incident and will most likely find that your clients' view of the situation is biassed by the trauma and is very negative. In other words, they usually believe the worst and react accordingly. During this stage you have the opportunity to look at different perspectives which could help them in their recovery. For instance, that the incident could have been far worse if they had not acted as they did. This is called reframing the incident.

'Reframing' their view of the situation

Reframing means that you introduce your clients to alternative scenarios or views of the situation to show that they acted correctly. In other words, that the outcome could have been far worse had they behaved any differently. You are trying to explain that their actions were well-thought out, considered, positive and appropriate under the circumstances. The idea is that by accepting a new view of the situation and their actions they change their negative beliefs about themselves and are able to let go of feelings of helplessness, losing control, guilt and self-blame.

Changing your clients' negative thinking

During this stage there is also a strong emphasis on changing your clients' thinking to lessen the effect of stressful or crippling emotions. This is done by challenging their negative thoughts (self-talk) one line at a time. Due to the effects of the trauma your clients' thinking is usually based on fallacies and inaccurate or exaggerated perceptions about their actions (or inactions) during the incident.

In this case you must become familiar with cognitive restructuring and how you can use this skill to help your clients. There are a number of ways of doing this. First, using the facts given to you in the earlier stages, you can offer them new insights into their actions.

Let us look at an example of how this is done, once again using the case study of Janet who, you may remember, was confronted by a knife-wielding man in her kitchen.

Case study

Janet believes that she was a helpless victim during the incident. She still remembers the feeling of being helpless and now days later, she is still not able to get her life back on track.

Counsellor: *'Janet, earlier you told me that you felt helpless during the incident.'*

Janet: *'Yes, I just stood there and did nothing.'*

Counsellor: *'But Janet is this entirely true?' 'What was the thought that went through your mind when you gave him your purse?'*

Janet: *'I suppose it was the thought that I must get him out of my kitchen as quickly as possible'.*

In this case you could point out to her that she acted with sound reasoning, deliberation and intent. This means that she was actually in control of her faculties and not as helpless as she believed. If she accepts this argument, she can replace her self-talk 'I was totally helpless' with 'I was not helpless.' 'I was thinking and in control of my decisions', and this should resolve, or at least reduce her feelings of helplessness and loss of control.

Using the benefit of hindsight

Second, using the benefit of hindsight and what could be considered reasonable and true, you can also show Janet that her perceptions of what she 'should' have done are unrealistic, not rational, in error, or not reasonable when viewed without bias.

Janet: *'I just stood there. I was so helpless.'*

Counsellor: *'Janet, in hindsight, don't you think that if you hadn't given him the bag he could have attacked you with the knife?'*

Janet: *'Yes, he threatened to do that.'*

Counsellor: *'So do you think it was unreasonable to have handed him the bag?'*

Janet: *'No, I suppose not. At least I got him out of there quickly.'*

Counsellor: *'So you actually acted with reason and were not helpless at all?'.*

OR

Janet: *'I just stood there. I was so helpless.'*

Counsellor: *'But Janet, that is not true. You consciously gave him the bag to get rid of him.'*

Janet: *'I suppose I did think to get him out of there quickly.'*

If Janet accepts your arguments it means that she can let go of her misguided perceptions and beliefs about her role in the incident and replace negative self-talk such as 'I was totally helpless' or 'I am a victim' with more positive statements such as 'I was not helpless', 'I got him out of there quickly' and be able to let go of her distressing emotions of helplessness and guilt.

Let us now also apply this skill once again to Peter's case study

Peter genuinely believes that he could have acted more with more courage during the hijacking by fighting back. But there is clear evidence that he may have been killed or seriously injured as a result. In this case you can also show that his belief is not rational or reasonable in view of the real-life situation.

Peter: *'I feel like I am a coward. I should have tackled him.'*

Counsellor: *'In hindsight, you told me that he already had the gun pointed at you. Do you think you would have been able to get to him before he pulled the trigger?'*

Peter: *'I don't think so. Now that I think about it, he stood a bit away from the car'*

Counsellor: *'Peter, you were clearly thinking and weighing up your chances. Under the circumstances, don't you think you did what any reasonable person would do.'*

Peter: *'I suppose so. It would have been a big risk and could have gone either way.'*

In this case, Peter's self-talk; 'I did nothing to stop the hijacking' ('and am therefore a coward'), can be replaced with; 'I did weigh up the situation. It would have been a big risk to get out of the car and tackle him.' I acted in the same way as any reasonable man under the circumstances' ('I am not a coward'). As a result, his feelings of guilt and self-blame should lessen and eventually fall away.

Showing them the power of having a plan

Another way of changing negative thinking is to show your clients that they were actively thinking and had some *plan of action* during the incident. Many negative self-beliefs relate to a perception that they were helpless and had no control over the situation. If you can find concrete examples to show that they, in fact, had a plan in mind (however simple), and acted according to this plan, they can regain their sense of being in control at the time and let go of the feeling of helplessness.

Once again, this means that you should point out any positive actions on the part of your clients during incidents.

If we use Janet's case study again, the fact that her children were at home was very important.

Counsellor: *'Janet, what was going through your mind about your children during all of this?'*

Janet: *'I was thinking that I have to get this person out of the kitchen as soon as possible to stop him harming the children'.*

Counsellor: *'So your plan was to give him the bag and get rid of him before he saw the children?*

Janet: *'Yes, I suppose I was thinking that.'*

Counsellor: *'So you were consciously thinking and had a plan to get rid of him quickly before he could harm the children?' 'Janet, you actually did very well to save the children. You were not helpless at all'*

Janet: *'You are right. I did plan to keep the robber away from the children'*

The idea of having had a plan shows clients that they were thinking and had at least some control over the situation. If they did something positive, such as in Janet's case, they can come to the understanding that their actions were correct and possibly even saved lives.

In other words, Janet can be shown that she did well, was not a helpless victim at all, was thinking clearly (although she was possibly not aware of this at the time), and was able to control the situation. This new insight can allow her to let go of the thoughts of being a helpless victim, the feelings of being helpless and can also return to her a sense of mastery and a more positive view of herself.

Praising your client

The idea of having a plan introduces the last strategy you can use to empower your clients during this stage, which is to praise them for any positive decisions they took and actions they carried out during the traumatic incident, even though, at the time, they may not have appeared important.

Once again using Janet's case study

Counsellor: *'So, by giving him your bag you were able to get him out of the kitchen speedily?'*

'That was quick thinking which could have saved your life'.

Janet: *'Yes, he ran away after that'*

Praise could be difficult in some cases in which your clients have had a hand in the traumatic incident, such as being the driver of a vehicle in which someone has been killed due to possible negligence. However, your commitment to your clients means that they get as much support from you as possible. Perhaps you can point out some mitigating factors. You can even just praise them for their courage in being prepared to work through the whole incident with you. It is very difficult to have to share your pain and feelings with others.

Identifying the turning point

What you are trying to bring about in stage four (empowerment) is a *turning point* for your clients, a moment at which they arrive at new, more positive insights about themselves and their actions, and are able to let go, or at least be able to manage, their remaining feelings of fear, helplessness, guilt and self-blame.

This turning point marks the time that they decide to take back their power from the aggressor and begin to have control over their lives again. It is the beginning of mastery.

STAGE 5: RETURNING A SENSE OF MASTERY TO YOUR CLIENTS

Mastery means that your clients have mastered the situation by being able to return to their normal day-to-day routine and functioning. This is the final phase of the trauma counselling process, namely *re-organisation* and *re-integration*, and this usually takes place during the third or fourth session, a few weeks after the incident.

This stage also involves a lot of thinking and discussion and assumes that your clients have let go of most of their intense emotions and feelings in earlier counselling sessions and are now coping quite well.

However, if you notice some remaining strong emotions, you must return to earlier stages and try to resolve them. Otherwise, if you feel that your clients are not responding well to counselling at all, refer them to specialists for more professional care. As I said, in my opinion, if they do not show any improvement after two or three sessions, this may mean they have already developed P.T.S.D or some other disorder which you are not qualified to treat.

So what is the process to be followed in this closing session?

Linking up and summarising what was said

Try to link up and summarise the progress made by your clients in earlier sessions. Specifically mention the *turning point* and the insights gained by your clients during the empowerment stage. Look at their present emotional state and self-talk to decide whether they ready to compile a plan for future mastery.

Counsellor: *'Carol, how are you feeling now? Are you ready to do your plan?'*

Looking at practical ideas to help your clients

This is the final stage of the trauma counselling process and you now need to help your clients put together a plan of action to bring their lives back on track and to cope with their outstanding concerns. This can be seen as a plan for mastery.

The plan must involve a number of practical ideas (action-steps) which will help them to cope day-to-day as well as in the future. This plan becomes a means for them to reclaim their personal power and regain the sense of once again being in control of their lives.

Each step should be carefully thought-out and discussed. You should try not to simply impose your ideas on your clients, even if you feel you are in a better position to advise them. The reason for this is that they need to accept ownership and responsibility for these ideas and decisions. In other words, your job is only to guide them through a decision-making process to select a series of options which are realistic, practical and workable within their frame of reference. In other words, any ideas included in the plan must take into consideration their real-life position, money situation, coping mechanisms, competencies and capabilities.

Helping your clients to compile a plan

The plan should be a collaborative effort between you and your clients. It should cover a number of important areas:

Looking at your clients' personal development

If your clients suffer from lack of self-confidence, self-esteem or coping skills, their plan should include steps to develop these skills and to rebuild their emotional wellness with a view to mastery.

Discuss suitable ideas to deal with these issues, such as courses teaching coping skills, emotional wellness or personal-growth.

Address their feelings of personal safety and security

The plan should also include solutions to ensure their personal safety and help them regain their feelings of security. Discuss security options that are available, such as lighting, safety doors, panic buttons, private security companies and armed response.

Looking for practical steps to provide social support

Also discuss practical steps to help your clients reconnect with their families and communities.

This can be done by involving their extended families in their lives and joining sports and social clubs, trauma support or church groups. Walking and yoga have been found to be great for stress relief. They could also find meaning in their lives by volunteering at many of the organisations helping animals, the elderly or vulnerable persons.

Encourage them to continue with, or take up creative hobbies such as art, writing and gardening.

They also need to look at their diets in order to eat healthy and remain positive.

Referring your clients for professional care

Include referrals to suitable professionals if your clients have any outstanding medical, legal or emotional concerns. Some clients who do not respond well to counselling could have underlying problems and may need medication or long-term therapy. You need to know your boundaries when it comes to trauma and have a resource book on hand in which you have listed the names and areas of expertise of different practitioners, support groups or recovery institutions if needed for referral to your clients.

Once you have agreed on the steps of the plan, encourage your clients to begin immediately. They should report back on the success of their plans during the last session which should be after about two weeks.

Motivating your clients

Sometimes bringing about changes to one's life can be a bit daunting. So you need to make sure that your clients are feeling fully empowered to go ahead with their plans. During this final stage of the counselling process you can change your voice, words and mood to inspire your clients and get them enthusiastic about the plan.

IMPLEMENTING THE PLAN

The final session

You can do the final (fifth) session either face-to face or online or by telephone if you feel that your client is doing well. During this session you should focus on how successful (or not) the plan has been and which steps have worked well and which have not. The plan can be changed at this time if necessary to include any new or more practical ideas. This will mean that there will have to be one more follow-up on the amended plan in a few weeks time.

If you find that your clients have not implemented their plan, it could be that they are confident enough to not worry about bringing about these extra changes to their lives, but it could also be that they still do not have the motivation and strength to do so. In this case you will need to look at their state of mind and make sure that they are fine emotionally and are coping well. If this is not the case do a bit more probing to discover the cause of the problem, or else refer them for more long-term counselling if it is not something you can deal with.

CONCLUSION

If you are successful with your trauma counselling, your clients should have renewed confidence and self-esteem, enhanced coping abilities and possibly even an improved resilience which will help them in facing future life-challenges.

Sometimes growth even takes place as a result of the incident and the counselling. Your clients have moved through a process of *self-discovery*, gained self-insight and are now able to recognise their true strengths and abilities. Having passed through the metaphorical '*valley of darkness*' their everyday problems may now seem insignificant.

You may also have benefitted from the counselling, in that you may have begun to develop your own counselling style that is more flexible and can be adapted to clients with different personalities and needs. Sometimes it is more important to develop a feel for the right approach rather than to get bogged down in a rigid structure and technicalities.

I wish you all the best for your future trauma counselling.

CHAPTER SIX

PRACTICAL ASSESSMENT

I have included this chapter on assessment for the purpose of using this guide for the training of lay counsellors or volunteers.

It is important to test would-be counsellors on their attitude, approach, knowledge of the process as well as their practical skills before allowing them to work with trauma. An improperly trained volunteer can do even more damage to an already traumatised person.

PRACTICAL TESTING

This chapter will show you how to test a group of trainees in practical counselling using role plays. You can check their theoretical knowledge either orally during interviews by talking about possible case studies, or by means of a written assignment.

CHARACTERISTICS OF A GOOD COUNSELLOR

The following aspects are important to decide if the trainee has the personality characteristics to make a good trauma counsellor. Their attitudes and personal attributes are just as important as their skills.

ASSESSMENT TABLE

Use a chart to see how they measure up on the following attributes:

If you wish you can design your own measuring sheet. This is just an example of an assessment chart. The following form is available for download at www.discovering yourself.co.za.

Trainee's name _____

Attitude	Unsatisfactory	Satisfactory	Good	Very good
Caring/ warmth				
Sensitivity				
Non-judgmental				
Listening skills				
Accurate reflection of feelings				
Accurate reflection of thoughts				
Empower-ment				
Option-handling				
Under-standing of the counselling process/ stages				

Assessed by   1. _____

2. _____

It is better to have two assessors in case there is a personal issue with a trainee.

Both assessors need to agree on the competency of the trainee. If there is doubt as to whether the trainee is suitable, the matter should be referred to a moderator for a decision.

HERE IS A DESCRIPTION OF WHAT IS REQUIRED FOR EACH ASPECT:

Attitude

Does the trainee show a genuineness and openness to learn and to help others?

Are they authentic and honest with themselves and others?

Caring and warmth

Does the trainee show empathy in their body language, their voice and choice of words?

Sensitivity

Does the trainee show moral or spiritual depth?

Non-judgmental

Does the trainee show unconditional acceptance of the client?

Does the trainee judge the client in any way?

Listening skills

Is the trainee able to keep a good focus on the client?

Do they apply the different listening skills correctly?

The accurate reflection of feelings

Is the trainee able to correctly identify, respond to and reflect feelings?

The accurate reflection of thoughts

Does the trainee show common sense, insight and understanding when identifying and reflecting the clients' thoughts?

Empowerment

Is the trainee able to effectively empower the client?

Option-handling

Is the trainee able to use a non-directive, logical, common-sense approach during option-handling and drawing up of a plan for mastery?

Understanding of the counselling process/ stages

Does the trainee show a good understanding of each stage of the trauma counselling process?

PRACTICAL TESTING USING ROLE PLAYS

This is a great and fun exercise for persons who love to act, as well as for those who have never done so, but would like the opportunity.

Separate your trainees into groups of three

Brief them beforehand as to what is expected of them.

One is to play the role of counsellor, one the role of a client, while the final trainee is an observer whose job it is to take notes and give feedback to the others after the exercise.

Prepare each trainee playing the client for the role they should play

They can be similar or different to the case studies already discussed in this guide. For example, a traumatised housewife confronted by an intruder, the victim of a hijacking, a mugging victim, a rape survivor, a person whose spouse suffered a violent death and so on. Use your imagination, but try to keep the role plays as close to real-life as possible.

Also coach the 'clients' before the time so that they know what you are looking for in each role play.

In other words, let one trainee play the role of a victim in great distress (impact phase), another a client in the recoil phase who does not really want to co-operate and another the survivor of past trauma (recovery phase).

Your job as the assessor is to walk in -between the different groups, quietly taking note of how each role play is being managed. In other words, does the trainee with the role of counsellor know the different skills and use them properly? You can use a marking schedule for this if you wish, but I find that taking obvious notes can make the trainees nervous and you may not get their best work.

Do role plays for each stage of the process (stage 1-5) so that the trainee has to show the skills for each different stage. If you wish you can prompt trainees who get 'stuck' in the process using a gesture, such as touching your chest for 'feelings' or your head for 'thoughts', or actually whispering guidance if they have left out important steps, but this means that they will have to be tested again on those aspects.

Each session should be about five to ten minutes, after which observers give feedback on aspects that need attention or steps that were left out, as well as praise for those areas in which the trainee did well. You as the assessor should also comment, give guidance and praise to each trainee plying the role of counsellor. Once this is done, the trainees switch roles and the process should be repeated.

Here are guidelines as to what to look for in each role play:

ROLE PLAY STAGE ONE

Let the trainees study the diagram and note the skills and processes required for stage one.

STAGE 1: BUILDING A RELATIONSHIP

The 'counsellor' and observer are already seated and the 'trauma-tised client' is brought in. The trainee playing the part of the client must be informed beforehand to act out the role of a badly trauma-tised person who is vulnerable and helpless and needs plenty of support and physical help.

These are the skills or outcomes you should be looking for:

Observing properly

The counsellor should immediately see the client's distress and get up, hold onto their arm and guide them to the chair.

As the client is clearly in the impact phase, once the client is sting down the 'counsellor' should sit close by in order to offer support. Female trainees (counsellors) can put their arms around the clients' shoulders or a hand on their arm but a male counsellor must be more careful where he puts his hand. He can reach out to touch her arm but if she pulls away he should not make further attempts to touch her. Discuss this 'acting' with the trainee playing the role of the client before the role play.

Identifying with the client

Counsellors should introduce themselves using a sympathetic and low voice tone, giving only their first names. This is to identify and to build rapport with the 'client'.

"I am James' 'I am a trauma counsellor and I'm here to help you'

The 'counsellors'' body language and demeanour should also show empathy and unconditional positive regard.

Reassuring the client

At this time the 'counsellor' should use small talk to put the 'clients' at ease and assure them that the session is confidential and they are there to help them through this incident. One of the ways the 'counsellor' should use to do this is to explain to them that the feelings, confusion and physical upsets they are having, are perfectly normal and to be expected in trauma.

Here are some possible words that they could use:

'This is normal for trauma and happens to everybody'.

'These are some of the symptoms you may experience in the next few days ...'.

'You will be lucky if you don't experience this'

The counsellor is not rushing through the process

Make sure that the 'counsellor' does not begin counselling immediately. These reassurances and feedback are necessary, as well as a few words of guidance before the real counselling begins.

The 'counsellors' may or may not encourage clients to return to work, depending on the given circumstances, but they should stress that 'clients' need to try and keep their routine as normal as possible, with help from family and friends. In this case it will be good if counsellors ask questions about the clients' support systems.

Fully informing the client

'Counsellors' should also inform the 'clients' not to take strong medication or alcohol, as this may slow down the process of recovery.

What you are looking for –a relationship of trust

What you as the assessor should be looking for in the stage one role play is a natural, flowing approach by the 'counsellor' in which the process is not rushed or forced. Look for this relationship in the way that the two interact and the 'clients' face expressions and body language show trust.

Discuss this acting with the trainee playing the client beforehand, so that he or she knows how to respond.

Review and feedback on stage one role play

Once you are satisfied, stop the role play (This usually takes about 2-3 minutes for stage one). There should have been no real counselling during this stage, only a show of compassion, support and reassurances with the 'counsellors' introducing themselves, reflecting a few words and asking only simple questions (small talk) about clients' family situations, how they are feeling and their concerns and medical problems, until the relationship of trust is there.

'Observers' now have to give feedback on what they have seen from the interaction between the 'counsellors' and 'clients'. You as the assessor need to add to this feedback. Try to keep it constructive and gently point out the most glaring mistakes. Trauma counselling is not easy and rather than being critical, you should try to empower and uplift the trainee as much as possible.

ROLE PLAY STAGE 2: EXPLORING EMOTIONS

Let the trainees study the handout again for stage for stage two

We are assuming the impact phase which is the worst case scenario.

These are the skills or outcomes you should be looking for:

The words used by each 'counsellor' can be different from the examples given but should have the same message.

Asking permission

The counsellor should give the client control of the situation

'If it is ok with you I am now going to ask you to tell me what happened'

'Is it alright if I ask you a few questions about what happened?'

Asking for a short version of the incident (he or she 'primes' the client)

Counsellor asks for the short version of what happened without too much focus on the feelings

'Before we go into all the details, just tell me briefly what happened.'

Uses euphemisms and past tense to distance clients from the incident

Asking permission again for in-depth exploration of feelings

Counsellor:

'Is it alright if I ask you some more questions about what happened?'

'This time will you tell me what you felt when these things happened?'

Using emotional distance

Counsellor:

'I don't' want you to relive it. Just tell me as if you are looking back at it.'

'I don't' want you to relive it. Just tell me what you remember'

'Think of it as a story you are telling me'

Reflecting each feeling or emotion

Counsellor uses listening skills (reflection) to reflect and fully explore each emotion as it comes out in the 'story.

Asking direct questions with empathy

Counsellor:

'What are you feeling?'

Identifying and naming the emotions.

Fear, terror, horror, guilt, helplessness or shame

Identifying the point or moment of trauma

Identifies the moment of trauma

Counsellor:

'What did you see that made you afraid?

'What did he say that made you afraid?

'What was the moment that you believed you were going to be killed?'

Counsellor spends time with emotions arising at this moment in time

Bringing on catharsis

Counsellor comforts, reflects and supports the client in distress. Clients shiver, shake, cry or sob to release body tension.

Review and feedback on stage two role plays

Once again observers give feedback on what they have seen from the interaction between the 'counsellors' and 'clients'. You as the assessor add to the feedback. As before, try to keep it constructive. Praise the 'counsellors' for good work done.

ROLE PLAY STAGE 3: EXPLORATION OF THOUGHTS

These are the skills and outcomes you should be looking for:

Asking permission

Counsellor gives clients control of the situation

'Is it alright if I ask you a few more questions, this time about what you were thinking?'

Reflecting thoughts or self-talk

Counsellor uses listening skills (reflection) to uncover and fully explore each thought as it comes out in the narrative.

Asking direct questions with empathy

Counsellor explores thoughts that emerged at the moment of trauma.

Client's thoughts and self-talk

'I am going to die'

'I will never see my children again'

'if only I had not driven along that road' (guilt)

Counsellor responds to emotional distress with empathy and support.

Identifying thoughts, incorrect perceptions and unhelpful beliefs for later restructuring

Counsellor uncovers clients' thoughts and self-talk (examples)

'I am going to die'

'I will never see my children again'

'if only I had not driven along that road' (guilt)

'I could have done more to prevent it'

'I should have fought back'

'It was my own fault'

Review and feedback on stage three role plays

As before, both you and the 'observers' give feedback. Remain positive.

ROLE PLAY STAGE 4: EMPOWERMENT

Let the trainees study the handout again for stage four

These are the skills and outcomes you should be looking for:

Remembering thoughts and beliefs from the previous stage

Counsellor is able to recall facts, as well as clients' emotions and thoughts from the previous stage.

Reframing thoughts to reduce emotions

Counsellor gives new perspectives of what could have happened using hindsight

Shows negative consequences of what could have happened

(far worse possible scenarios)

Counsellor shows that their concerns (guilt, etc) are not rational

'So from what you have told me it would not have been a good idea to push the button?'

Reinforcing what they did as right and correct.

Counsellor: *'So by keeping quiet you actually saved your life?*

Challenging with empathy

Counsellor points out negative thoughts and unhelpful beliefs

Counsellor uses hindsight to logically look at clients' actions or non-actions and refute thoughts and self-talk using reason, common sense, truth and actual circumstances.

Counsellor:

'And then ..? What could have happened if you had done ...this or that?'

'Was what you did not reasonable under the circumstances?

'The truth of the matter was that you had no other option'

Tries to help client let go of self-destructive thoughts and beliefs

Guiding client to more positive thoughts and view of self

Counsellor shows clients they were thinking rationally and had a PLAN

'So your plan was to...?'

Counsellor gives support and praise to clients' actions at the time

Counsellor leads clients to understand and accept that what they did was good.

Counsellor brings about a **turning poin**t at which time clients change their self-talk and beliefs.

Using other empowerment techniques

Counsellor discusses other techniques to reduce tension such as relaxation and visualisation

Review and feedback on stage four role plays

As before, both you and the 'observers' give feedback.

ROLE PLAY STAGE 5: MASTERY

Let the trainees study the handout again for stage for stage five

These are the skills and outcomes you should be looking for:

Helping clients look at options to bring normality to their lives

Counsellor helps client to explore ideas to deal with security, legal, health and social concerns

(Eliciting family, social and community support)

Counsellor is non-directive; the decisions are the 'clients'

End-result is a set of practical, realistic and achievable options for each concern

Helping clients to compile a plan for mastery

Counsellor helps client to look at practical, realistic and achievable options and to formulate them into plans with action steps (Plans have steps for reconnecting with family and friends)

Counsellor helps with ideas for personal growth (life-coaching or personal growth courses), for exercise, relaxation, improved diet, sports, hobbies, volunteer work (to keep clients busy)

Counsellor make referrals for long-term assistance (medical, emotional, legal)

Counsellor strives for improved resilience in client

CONCLUSION

Motivating client to go ahead with plan

Counsellor summarises what has been achieved and praises client for completing the process and the plan.

ARRANGING FOLLOW-UP SESSIONS TO CHECK ON PLAN

Sum up the counsellor's abilities and make recommendations for selection.

It is also a good idea to have a selection panel of more than one person for choosing counsellors. Only one person selecting could be open to accusations of bias.

PART TWO

Case studies of trauma counselling

INTRODUCTION

Welcome to part two of Trauma Counselling: A practical guide to dealing with Trauma. As with part one, this guide has been specially prepared for care-givers, lay-counsellors and the training of lay counsellors. Part one gave you a basic understanding of trauma and trauma skills and this guide follows on by exploring a number of case-studies to show you how the skills are used in practice. Some of the case studies are based on real-life interventions. Due to confidentiality, the names and some details have been changed. However, this is what you can expect in practice. Tips for running a community counselling centre can also be found in the different descriptions.

Notice that the counselling process in these case studies is divided up into different sessions. This is normally the case. However, if the trauma is long past and your client is not in any distress, you may be able to work through the process in a single counselling session.

The case studies are shortened for practical reasons. They would normally take one to two hours. Only the key steps and most important areas in each case are shown and not the whole process. If you would like more information on each step, read this guide together with part one, which is more detailed.

I hope that these case studies will show you how trauma counselling is done in real-life settings by lay counsellors, and that this will make the steps and skills much clearer.

Best wishes

Jimmy Henderson Ph.D (Psychology)

CHAPTER ONE

THE 5 STAGE COUNSELLING PROCESS

Please refer to the diagram of a simple structured, outcomes-based trauma counselling process consisting of five stages as shown on (p96, Part 1) that highlights the different skills needed at each stage.

THE STAGES GIVEN ARE:

Stage one: Build a good relationship with your clients

Stage two: Explore your clients' feelings and emotions

Stage three: Explore your clients' thinking

Stage four: Empower your clients to cope

Stage five: Return a sense of mastery to your clients

Stages one to three would be suitable for the impact and recoil phases of the trauma process and stages four and five for the third and final phase of re-organisation and re-integration. In this regard I suggest that you read through the chapters on 'What is trauma' and 'The different phases of Trauma' in part one.

As we work through these case studies, I will mention the chapters and sections in part one where you can get more information on the particular skill or aspect of the counselling. It would therefore be a good idea to have part one with you when you study this guide

CHAPTER TWO

HOW TO DEBRIEF GROUPS

In part one I make it clear that *debriefing* is not the same as trauma counselling. Debriefing is a shortened process which is usually given to groups of traumatised workers (or survivors) as a first line of counselling. In other words, it is meant to help persons exposed to a traumatic event which need immediate support when time is limited and the logistics for one-on-one trauma counselling is not available. Trauma counselling is a much longer and more thorough process in which each person is given special attention. Group debriefing also helps the counsellor decide which members of the group are the most traumatised and will need one-on-one counselling.

Usually, a counsellor takes a group of not more than eight persons for debriefing (a maximum of ten), as with more the process will become too time-consuming and unwieldy.

If there many people needing debriefing, such as at the scene of a natural or man-made disaster, they should be divided into groups of eight and a number of different trauma counsellors used. In emergencies one counsellor can make arrangements to debrief different groups one after another. However, this is very demanding on the counsellor and is also a problem for those who have to wait in line for attention, as it is not a good idea to leave traumatised people alone without support.

Also, if there is a language problem, you can arrange for an interpreter to assist you. With group debriefing this is easier, as it is more open and flexible than a closed counselling session. Having an assistant may also be a good idea if there are cultural differences that need to be kept in mind.

CASE STUDY OF A GROUP DEBRIEFING PROCESS

This case study is based on an actual event which involved a group of workers in a large retail store traumatised by an armed robbery.

Group debriefing has a few logistical problems and your needs for privacy and a suitable room will need to be discussed with the store manager.

SETTING UP

In this case study, the counsellor, John, asked the store manager to arrange for the traumatised workers to be put in a large, private room away from the sales area with no interruptions. John is a male counsellor and this presents some problems for the debriefing of female workers, as will be seen later.

John asks the manager not to be at the debriefing, only the workers affected by the robbery. This helps with confidentiality, as a manager being there may stop the workers from sharing their true feelings and concerns. If managers were directly involved in the incident and are also traumatised, they could form part of the group, but would then have to commit to strict confidentiality regarding the session. Usually managers are counselled separately as there are extra issues involved, as will be seen later.

INTRODUCTION (STAGE ONE)

John has asked the manager to provide a private space and enough chairs so that the workers can sit in a semi-circle. He himself sits facing the group.

NOTE:

If you are called out to an airport or other place which does not have loose chairs, you will have to place the people together as best you can so that they form a group. This is important, because in an emergency call-out to a disaster there will be many groups with counsellors and privacy and noise could be a problem. Groups must sit in such a way so that they do not interfere with each other.

Let us return to the case study of John debriefing the employees at the large retail store.

John makes sure that all the workers are properly seated in a semi-circle facing him. This allows him to engage with each one face-to-face. He then introduces himself to the group. A manager could also do the introduction, but should then leave the room. As mentioned, workers will not feel comfortable with a manager present.

Counsellor: 'Hi everyone. My name is John. I am a trauma counsellor and have been asked by the company to help you'.

It is a good idea to always use first names to 'break the ice', create a positive first impression, and set the tone for forming a relationship of trust with the group.

John begins by assuring them that the debriefing is confidential and that anything they say during the session will not be passed onto management. John also asks that the members of the group not give out any personal information shared by the others during the session. This will especially be the case if a supervisor is in the group. Once they commit to this, John explains the debriefing process.

John sets the rules and boundaries for the debriefing. He explains how he will ask each member of the group in turn to briefly speak about their experience, what they saw, heard or felt during the incident. He asks that the workers allow each other the time to speak and try not to dominate the group process. He also asks that they support each other.

John now *normalises* their feelings, which include shock, fear, confusion and helplessness, as well as medical issues such as headaches and nausea. He explains to them that these symptoms are all natural and normal for what they have experienced. Some workers ask him questions about the symptoms, which he answers. This reassurance is meant to put the group at ease and help them to feel more in control.

After this, John believes he has the trust and confidence of the group and begins the debriefing process (stage two of the process)

For a group debriefing you can decide on either a structured or a less-structured approach.

A structured approach means that you will begin at one end of the group (from left to right, or right to left) and spend time with each person in turn, giving each a certain amount of time (five to ten minutes) to share with the group. If it is a group of eight, this means a total time of one hour, which is fine for a group debriefing, as by this time some of the members will need personal counselling.

If you decide on a less-structured approach, this means opening the floor to the group and inviting them to share spontaneously. The structured approach is probably better for children who may not have the self-discipline to give each other a turn. Adults should be able to understand and keep to the rules of a less structured process. However, in any event, a useful guideline is always to begin with those members who seem the most upset and traumatised.

As mentioned in part one of this series, the ideal distance for face-to-face counselling is about one to one-and-a-half meters. However, in the case of group debriefing you will sit a few meters away, facing them at a distance from which you can engage them all. However, if any member breaks down and needs support, you move your chair closer to the normal counselling distance so that you can comfort and give this group member your personal attention.

THE PROCESS OF EXPLORING FEELINGS AND THOUGHTS (STAGES TWO AND THREE)

John decides to use an unstructured process and opens the floor by posing a few questions about the incident to the whole group. They seem quite willing to share their stories on the incident and take turns to explain how they experienced it. As a result, he is able to recreate the event in his mind, which provides him with a useful framework for his later debriefing.

With group members now beginning to spontaneously share their emotions and thoughts, John reflects and notes each one's reactions and body-language. Due to the amount of workers in the group, John sets time limits for each person, with the result that his reflection and exploration of feelings, thoughts and concerns is not as comprehensive as it would be with one-on-one trauma counselling. Proper trauma counselling will be given to those who are worst affected after the group process.

John listens and acknowledges all their experiences and feelings as important, even those which seem trivial. As they begin to share their stories, out of the corner of his eye (using peripheral vision), John sees that some workers in the group are becoming very distressed. He waits for a suitable moment and excuses himself and moves his chair closer to a female employee who is leaning forward with her head in her hands. Her body-posture suggests a high level of anxiety and she seems quite helpless. During the open session of sharing he had noticed that she did not speak at all.

John engages her in a particularly empathetic and non-judgemental manner, asking her name and work position in the store. She gives her name as Susan and she is a cashier. He gently questions her about her experience of the incident, using simple counselling skills such as listening and reflection. She is clearly in distress. John asks if she can give her feelings of anxiety a number out of ten, to which she replies an eight (8). This takes her mind off the incident for a few moments and allows John to give her back her sense of control. He does this by reassuring her that if she feels anxiety with a rating of nine or ten coming on, she must tell him and he will stop and give her time to recover.

John also places her at an emotional distance from the incident by asking her not to relive the incident but to try and take a step back, as the incident is in the past.

John: *'What do you remember from your experience?'*

Susan: *'The robber was right next to me'*

John: '*And what did you feel at the time?'*

Susan: *'I was in a panic and terribly afraid'*

At this point Susan begins to cry and show stronger emotions. John immediately leans towards her to show support and uses empathetic words.

John: *'I understand that this must be very difficult for you. Take your time.'*

She again places her head in her hands and falls forward towards him. This could mean that she would welcome physical support and John reaches out and places his hand on her back.

As shown in part one, it is best for a male counsellor to only place his hand on a female client's shoulder or back if he feels that she would be open to his touch. Any other place on her body could make her uncomfortable or feel threatened. If Susan tenses up or pulls away, John would have to back off immediately. However, John interprets the fact that she falls forward towards him as a cue that she would welcome a soothing touch, and in this case, it is correct, as Susan does not pull away but continues to sob, and John moves his hand to her shoulders.

Susan is too upset and not able to carry on with her story, and another woman in the group, who had earlier identified herself as Anne and is sitting next to Susan, tells the group that there was a confrontation between Susan and the gunman. She explains how Susan was directly threatened with a gun and forced to open the till.

This gives Susan the time to compose herself again and in a few moments she continues sharing her experience with the group, who all respond with empathy and words of support.

Using listening and reflection skills, John helps Susan identify and acknowledge intense feelings of fear and helplessness. She expresses these feelings while being supported by John as well as the whole group. It often happens that the less traumatised members of a group help the others.

As I said earlier, it is not a good idea to give all the attention to any one member of the group, as this will use up all the available time and others may not get the time they need to share their own stories. I would recommend about five to ten minutes for each member of the group. So while he is busy with Susan, John notices that another member of the group, a male worker named James, is vomiting into his handkerchief, so he asks Anne to support Susan while he attends to James. You will find that some persons in the group, even though they have also been exposed to the same terrible situation, are more resilient and able to show empathy and support other members.

John: *'Anne, will you look after Susan for a short while?' 'I will get back to her as soon as I can.'*

Susan is clearly not settled and will need one-on-one counselling, so before he moves across to James, John asks her to come for counselling after the debriefing session.

John now moves his chair and shifts his attention to James, who is shaking and still vomiting. He engages James in the same way as Susan, showing empathy and unconditional positive regard.

John encourages him to share his experience of the incident briefly and what he is feeling and thinking.

James explains that he was also directly threatened with a gun by another robber and believed at the time that he was going to be shot and killed. He cannot get the sight of the gun out of his mind or shake off the feelings of panic and fear. John helps him to talk about the experience and his feelings of panic and fear at the moment of trauma (the sight of the gun and the thought that he would be killed).

After sharing this harrowing information with the group and getting their sympathy and support, James wipes his eyes a few times and seems more relaxed. There is a lot of power in the group giving support to a group member. It helps them feel they are not alone in this horrible experience.

However, James has been exposed to a violent threat and is clearly showing trauma symptoms, so John asks him to also come for face-to-face trauma counselling after the session. James is still shaking and this means that his body is struggling to let go of the stress. As part of his treatment John will refer James for a course of T.R.E (Tension, Stress and Trauma release) with a qualified practitioner which is designed to bring on natural tremors in the body in a controlled and sustained way. This is said to be able to release the deep muscular tension from trauma held in the body.

John now thinks James is reasonably stable and turns his attention back to the rest of the group.

None of the group seems to be in severe distress and they have stopped talking, but not everyone has had a chance. So John begins a more structured approach, starting with the worker on the far right of the group and moving left, using the same listening and reflection skills as before for each in turn. As before, each group member is given the opportunity to share feelings, thoughts and concerns with the group for a few minutes and receive John's full attention.

When John reaches Susan and James again, he asks whether they are still coping before moving on to the next worker. It seems that they are managing with the support of their friends in the group, but will still need one-on-one counselling. As he finishes his process with the group, John does notice that some workers were not directly exposed to the robbery and seem fine. However, he identifies those who do need further in-depth trauma counselling and asks them to stay behind after the debriefing.

It happens sometimes that workers not directly involved in the incident will not need one-on-one counselling, although it is still advisable to check up on them during the debriefing as well as in the days following. The company will often want follow-up sessions, especially with those workers that are badly traumatised. Make sure that the manager gives you a list of all the workers you debrief so that you can follow up later.

EMPOWERMENT OF THE GROUP (STAGE FOUR)

This is sometimes called the *learning* stage in group debriefing. After spending an hour dealing with the feelings , thoughts and experiences of each group member, John is now ready to give out important information about what they can expect in the next few days, as well as ways of coping. In other words, the workers need to be empowered to help them adjust to their experiences over the next few days and to try to reclaim control of their lives.

John adds to the information he gave earlier when he *normalised* their symptoms and responses.

He tells them to expect problems with sleeping and possibly having nightmares about the incident. John warns further that these symptoms could get worse. The negative feelings and thoughts will probably carry on for the next few days as well as flashbacks (images) of the event. They will most likely also have a range of physical symptoms such as headaches, nausea or diarrhoea, and any medical conditions they already have will probably get worse.

They may have problems at work with concentration, but he encourages them not to stay alone at home or take too much sick leave, as they will need help and support over the next few days. John also warns them not to use strong alcohol or medication, as this may delay their recovery.

He tells them about ways of coping and letting go of the traumatic stress, such as spending time with friends, listening to music, exercising and keeping busy with hobbies and other fun activities. It is always a good idea if a friend or family member spends a few days with a traumatised person so that they are not left alone with their negative feelings and thoughts.

By *priming* them for these likely responses and giving them ways of coping, John hopes to lessen their stress, confusion and feelings of a loss of control. John warns them that if their symptoms do not get better they should report to their HR department and be sent to a doctor or psychologist for long-term treatment.

Those identified for one-on-one counselling will be seen by John and watched over closely in the next few days.

CLOSURE

It is not possible to go to stage five (mastery) in one session when debriefing a group of workers that have been traumatised. Getting to this stage takes time. The stage of mastery with option-handling and a recovery plan will apply to those that have one-on-one counselling with John, and they will need to have a number of trauma sessions to recover fully. John will simply follow up on the others who coped well in the next few days to make sure that they are still fine.

In closing, John links and summarises the experiences of the group which they have shared, normalising their feelings and thoughts on the matter. He also allows for questions from the group about their immediate concerns for safety in view of the robbery that has taken place.

ASSURANCES

To answer these questions John invites the store manager into the room. The manager gives the group assurances regarding their safety. He tells them that security will be increased and a panic-button system installed at all cash register points. He also offers follow-up services to the group in the form of medical treatment and long-term professional counselling and also answers a number of other questions relating to after-hours shifts, which is also seen as a security concern.

After the manager has left, John thanks the group for their participation and once again assures them that the session was confidential. After leaving the room he discreetly gives the manager a list of employees that need immediate one-on-one trauma counselling after the debriefing. He is careful not to give any personal details shared by group members during the session.

ADDITIONAL NOTES

A group debriefing process is therapeutic in that those affected come to realise that being caught up in the same situation, they all share the same feelings and thoughts. This binds them together. However, it cannot replace one-on-one counselling which takes place over a few weeks.

The group debriefing process should not be longer than one or two hours, as badly traumatised members will need one-on-one counselling by this time. More group debriefing sessions can be arranged if the company requests it, but personal counselling for each person is the better option.

If you are debriefing a church group or members of a religious community where one or more of their members have been killed in an incident, I have found it useful to close the debriefing session with a prayer or even arrange with their minister for an impromptu church service.

CHAPTER THREE

ONE-ON-ONE COUNSELLING

As I showed in part one of the series, proper trauma counselling cannot be done in one session. It is a long process of many weeks which changes as the person begins to work through the trauma, fear and pain with the help of the counsellor. This can be clearly seen the following example which acts as a case study for the one-on-one counselling of a client at a community counselling centre.

THE CASE STUDY OF JANE

THE CASE BACKGROUND

It is a good idea if the counsellor has a basic idea outline of the incident and type of trauma before the counselling takes place. This is not always possible, but certainly helpful, as will be seen in this example. This information can be given to the office by the family member of friend who makes the arrangements.

In this case study a single mother, Jane, was threatened with a gun by an intruder and robbed in her kitchen while her children were in the playroom watching television. She is very traumatised and unable to drive. She has been brought to the counselling centre by her older sister Dorothy who arranged the counselling session with the centre over the phone.

INITIAL CONTACT

A reception clerk meets Jane and Dorothy in a friendly manner and guides them to a waiting room, as the counsellor on duty, Mary, is not available immediately. In the meantime, Jane's personal details are recorded by the reception clerk. This information is kept confidential in a locked cabinet in the reception room.

The counselling room is separate from the waiting room and quite private, away from busy office activities to keep the noise level down and interruptions to a minimum. It has a subdued colour scheme, soft lighting, comfortable furniture and a layout suitable for face-to-face counselling. The temperature in the room is also regulated.

SESSION ONE

The counsellor (Mary) comes out of the counselling room and tells the reception clerk that she is ready for Jane, who, together with her sister, is then taken by the clerk into the room.

In cases of severe trauma it is a good idea if a close friend or family member is also present during a face-to-face counselling session. This person can give added support as well as details which the traumatised person may be too upset to remember.

In cases where a woman has been sexually assaulted by a man, it will also be a good idea to have a second (female) counsellor helping as well, as the female client, under the circumstances, may be reluctant to speak freely to a male counsellor.

INTRODUCTION (STAGE ONE)

Mary meets Jane and Dorothy at the door and asks the clerk to make sure that the session is not disturbed or interrupted in any way.

It is clear from her body language and facial expressions that Jane is in the *impact or acute phase* and is having many of the emotions and responses normally associated with trauma such as fear, disorientation and helplessness.

Mary takes Jane's arm and guides her to the couch. Dorothy sits next to Jane on the couch and holds her tightly. Mary seats herself in a chair a little way across from the couch, close enough to reach out and touch Jane should the need arise, but not close enough to make her uncomfortable.

Mary begins by informing Jane of the confidentiality of the session and briefly engages her in small talk to help her relax. A trauma counselling session should not be rushed, especially in the case of a very distressed client.

Mary: *'I understand that you have three children and stay in Westville?'*

Jane: *'Yes, they are nine, ten and twelve years old'*

Mary: *'Is someone looking after them at the moment?'*

Jane: *'Yes, my mother has come over and is taking care of them'.*

Mary then asks Jane if she is having any symptoms such as nausea, diarrhoea or headaches. Jane answers 'yes', she has stomach pains and has been vomiting. She is also having panic attacks and the whole situation feels out of control. Mary empathises with her and reassures her that this is normal under the circumstances. She explains that her panic attacks, as well as intense feelings of fear and helplessness could carry on for a few days still or even weeks. Mary has now warned Jane in advance and hopefully Jane will not be confused when this happens. This should lessen her panic attacks and her sense of losing control.

Mary briefly outlines the process she will be following with Jane, a short factual account followed by a deeper exploration of her feelings and thoughts about the incident. She tells Jane that she will not be asked to relive the situation, but rather to see it as something that happened in the past, a series of unpleasant memories. Mary then asks Jane's permission to begin and assures her that she can pause or stop at any time, but also warns her that she may be interrupted to clarify certain issues. Giving Jane this information allows her a sense of control and is aimed at lessening her anxiety and stress.

However, it is clear that Jane is still not able to relax and Mary asks her if she can try an exercise to help her. Jane agrees and using a quiet and subdued tone of voice, Mary guides her through a brief muscle relaxation exercise in which she is asked to close her eyes, sit quietly and begin to breathe deeply and regularly. Jane must also try to imagine a wave of peace slowly moving up from her feet, though her ankles and legs, into her hips, over her chest and up her backs. Mary tells her to concentrate on her breathing and the imagined movement through her body and at the same time, to empty her mind of all thoughts until it is completely quiet.

This exercise appears to have helped as Mary sees from Jane's body-language that she is starting to relax. This also means that she now trusts Mary and that a good relationship has been built.

NOTE:

This exercise is fully described in part one of this guide.

Mary then asks Jane to tell her briefly what happened at her home. She reflects a few words to clarify some facts, but does not ask Jane about her emotions and feelings at this time.

Jane explains that she was in the kitchen when an intruder entered unexpectedly and demanded money. She remembers the intruder pointing a gun at her, and indicating to him that her handbag was on the table. Jane admits to being very afraid and becomes very emotional when she speaks of the gun.

EXPLORING FEELINGS AND THOUGHTS (STAGES TWO AND THREE)

Mary stops and allows Jane a few moments to compose herself. During this time she is hugged by her sister and comforted by Mary who has now leant forward to place her hand on Jane's arm as a gesture of support.

Having obtained the facts of the incident and identifying the moment of trauma as the sight of the gun, Mary waits for Jane to recover before starting with stages two and three of the counselling process, exploring these crippling feelings and thoughts.

After a minute or two of crying Jane appears to have settled down Mary asks her if she can carry on. Jane nods. Jane begins to tell her story again, but this time Mary reflects her feelings as they come out. She also asks more questions about the intruder's actions, her feelings each step of the way and the kind of thoughts that passed through her mind. She reminds Jane to try to distance herself from the incident by seeing it as something that is in the past, as she is now safe.

As mentioned, from Jane's responses, Mary believes the sight of the gun to be the moment of trauma, the point at which Jane went into shock and had those feelings of total loss of control and helplessness. She also tells Mary that that was the moment she thought she was going to die.

Mary explores this moment on detail:

Mary: *'You mentioned that at that moment you felt afraid and completely helpless?'*

Jane: *'I can't describe the feeling fully. I went into shock and was crippled by a sudden fear of dying'*

Mary: '*And at that point you thought you were going to die?*'

Jane: *'Yes, and all I could think about was what is going to happen to my children'.*

Mary: *'That must have been the worst fear for you*' (reflection)

Jane: '*Yes, my first thought was to get him out of here'.*

Notice how Jane's feelings and thoughts and Mary's skills of listening and reflection merge and flow in one continuous process.

Mary continues to explore Jane's emotions in depth. However, to prevent re-traumatisation, she phrases the questions in such a way as to create an emotional distance between Jane and the full horror of the trauma.

Mary: *'Tell me more about when you felt that feeling of helplessness.'*

Jane: *'It felt like I was frozen to the spot. I did not even think of doing anything'*

Mary: *'You felt that you had no control?'* (reflection)

Jane: *'Yes, all I wanted to do was get him out of the house.'*

While sharing this part of the incident, even with the 'emotional distance', Jane's emotions are so intense that she once again breaks down and is hugged by her sister and comforted by Mary, who now shifts her chair closer, holds Jane's hand and stops counselling.

Mary encourages her to allow herself to experience the emotions now, as she is loved and supported. After shivering and crying for a short while, much of the tension has left Jane's body and she is ready to carry on.

(Note that if the counsellor is male the touching of the hand of a female client is not advised).

Once Jane has composed herself, Mary identifies and reflects Jane's other intense emotions and opens up her self-talk with each emotion. Mary encourages cathartic release by giving her ongoing empathetic support during emotional moments, but also makes a mental note of the thoughts that Jane was having with each emotion. Mary can see that Jane is very fearful, and Jane admits that she also feels helpless and a little guilty at not having done more to stop the intruder from getting into the kitchen.

After about an hour Mary sees that Jane is exhausted and decides to end the first session. She tells Jane that the counselling sessions will need to continue tomorrow and takes time to list other typical symptoms that she might have during the night. Mary also asks that Jane's sister Dorothy stay with her for a few days to assist her with household chores as well as the statements that she needs to make to the police. She also recommends that Jane consults her doctor for treatment for the upset stomach she is experiencing.

Mary ends by assuring Jane that she is with her every step of the way and hugs both Jane and her sister Dorothy. She accompanies them to the reception area where they make arrangements for the next appointment. As Jane is in the impact phase, this will have to be the next morning (within twenty-four hours after the incident).

SESSION TWO

The next morning Dorothy brings Jane to the counselling centre for the second session. They are again greeted at the door by Mary who guides them to the couch where Jane and her sister sit next to each other. Mary notices that Jane is still nervous and anxious, although more relaxed than she was the day before. She hopes that Jane has been able to move into the recoil phase.

Mary begins by asking Jane if she coped last night and what symptoms she had. Jane replies that she had a restless night and did not sleep well at all. Mary assures her that this is perfectly normal in view of what has happened to her.

Mary then asks Jane to share any images, dreams, feelings or thoughts she had during the night. Jane's persistent feelings of fear and anxiety and the flashbacks (vivid images of the incident in the kitchen) that she remembers from the night before, do concern Mary and she explores these further using reflection and questioning. Once again, Jane becomes emotional when she speaks about her emotions and is comforted by Mary as well as her sister, Dorothy. Once again Mary tells her to allow herself to feel the emotions and to release the tension from her body through the sobbing and shivering.

EMPOWERMENT (STAGE FOUR)

After a while Jane has settled down and admits that she is feeling better and less emotional. Mary now decides that they are now ready to move to the next stage of the trauma counselling process, '*empowerment*'. During this stage the focus will be on Jane's negative thinking and beliefs as seen in her self-talk.

Mary recalls Jane's self-talk around the moment of trauma from the previous session and asks her to clarify or acknowledge her thoughts as she remembers them. Mary tries to link each of the lines of self-talk to the actions that took place during the incident. She notices that Jane has now been able to distance herself somewhat from the incident by speaking about it in a more detached way, more like a narrative. Once a client can do this, they are on their way to recovery.

Mary is pleased that Jane is now in the *recoil* phase of the trauma process. This means that her emotional state is more balanced and Mary will be able to begin to challenge the self-talk which is feeding Jane's distressing emotions.

During her questioning, Mary sees that Jane's feeling of helplessness is based on the thought that she believed that she was powerless to do anything to help herself. She is also blaming herself for not having done more to stop the robbery, such as having the back door locked, or pushing the intruder out of the kitchen.

Mary gently challenges this line of thinking, pointing out that it is not unusual for people to leave their back-doors open during the day, due to chores such as sweeping, hanging up the washing and gardening. In other words, she shows Jane that it was not unreasonable or irrational for her to have left the door open and unlocked at that time. Jane seems relieved to see that the counsellor supports what she did.

Mary now tackles Jane's belief that she could have done more to help herself by pushing the intruder out of the kitchen and locking the door. She does this by using the benefit of hindsight and reframing the incident to show Jane that the outcome could have been far worse if she had acted on this thought and not in the manner that she did, which was to remain calm and point to her bag. In this way Mary hopes to remove Jane's feelings of guilt and self-blame arising from the incident.

Mary: *'Jane, you told me that the intruder was a large man and had a gun pointed at you.'*

Jane: *'Yes, that is correct'.*

Mary: *'In the light of what you have just told me, what could have happened if you had gone for him or even pushed him?'*

Jane: *'I suppose he could have hit me with the gun or even shot me'*

Mary: *'Don't you think your decision to give him your bag was the right one, as he left straight away?'*

Jane: *'I suppose so'*

At this time Jane starts sobbing again. Hopefully this is from relief at having let go of the thought of blaming herself. Mary responds with empathy and a gentle tone of voice and uses kind words to comfort her. She reflects Jane's emotions as they emerge, helping her once again to feel them but then to let go. After Jane has relaxed again, Mary carries on examining Jane's self-talk which she believes is feeding those distressing emotions.

Mary now focuses on Jane's most powerful emotion, which is fear. Jane previously mentioned that the image of the gun and the thought that she was going to die kept her awake during the night. Mary decides that this terrible fear arose when Jane saw the gun. This was the moment of trauma.

Mary approaches this line of self-talk this head on.

Mary: *'Yesterday, you told me that at that moment you thought you were going to die?'*

Jane: *'Yes, all I could think about was my children and what would happen to them'*

Mary: *'So your main concern was your children?'*

Jane: *'Yes; and that I was powerless to protect them'*

Mary can now see that Jane's fear and feelings of helplessness arose from the belief that she was powerless in the situation and had lost her ability to protect herself and her family. Mary decides to use *cognitive restructuring* to attack this belief as misguided and to show Jane that she was, in fact, thinking clearly, acting according to a plan of action and had control over the situation.

Mary: *'What else did you think at the time?'*

Jane: *'I thought that I must get this person out of the house as quickly as possible'*

Mary: *'This is important, so your plan at the time was to give the intruder your bag and get him out of the house as soon as possible?*

Jane: *'Yes, that's true.'*

Using the benefit of the benefit of hindsight, Mary attempts to *deconstruct* Jane's earlier belief that she was powerless and to show her that she was, in fact, not a helpless victim during the incident.

Mary: *'From what you said, you were thinking clearly at the time. You were not helpless. You had a plan to get him out of the house and away from the children as quickly as possible'*

Jane: *'I suppose that is true.'*

Mary: *And part of your plan was to point to your bag, which he took and ran out.*

Jane: *'Yes'*

Mary: *'So in fact, you actually controlled the situation and were not helpless at all?'*

Jane: *'Yes, I suppose now that I was not as helpless as I believed. I was able to save my children.'*

Mary notes a positive shift in Jane's body-language which shows that she has responded well to this new insight and understanding.

Mary continues to praise Jane for her actions during the incident, helping her *reconstruct* her self-talk into more positive self-truths and rebuild her shattered self-esteem. These new insights and feelings of competency should counter the fear linked to the misguided belief in her powerlessness and (perceived) loss of control.

Based on changes in Jane's body-language and tone of voice, Mary feels that she has achieved her objective in this second session, that is, to change Jane's self-talk to a more positive direction.

All that Jane needs now is time to adjust a bit more before they look at practical steps to return her life to normality. Before she leaves, Mary gives Jane an exercise called a relaxation meditation to try at home which is also fully explained in part one of this guide. The exercise is designed to help her body get rid of the tension that goes with trauma.

To show Jane how it is done, Mary guides her through it once.

Mary tells Jane to sit quietly and comfortably, close her eyes and begin breathing to a slow count of one to five. She must focus on nothing else but the counting. Mary guides Jane as she breathes in and out. 'Breathe in 1,2,3,4,5, hold your breath, 1,2,3,4, 5, breathe out 1,2,3,4,5, hold your breath 1,2,3,4,5, breathe in 1,2,3,4,5'. She tells Jane to carry on with the counting and breathing until her mind is quiet and she feels more relaxed. After each cycle Mary asks Jane to rate how she is feeling on a scale of one to ten. She is looking for an improvement in Jane's body-tension. Apart from Jane's feedback, the lessening of her tension can be seen in changing body language.

Mary encourages Jane to try this exercise at home and build on what she has achieved in this session. She is told to come for the next session in three days. After hugging both Dorothy and Jane, Mary takes them to the reception room where Jane makes the appointment.

SESSION THREE

If all has gone well, by the third session clients should be emotionally quite stable and so the focus can shift to further empowering them to reclaim control of their lives and to manage their emotions and thoughts on a day-to-day basis.

This time Jane is alone. Mary greets her at the door and guides her to the couch. As before, Mary sits across from her about one to one-and--a-half meters away and notices from her reasonably relaxed tone of voice and body-language that she is coping much better.

Mary once again begins the session with light conversation, asking how Jane's children are coping and if she has gone back to work. Mary praises Jane for the manner in which she has coped by herself in the days before this session and asks about her earlier symptoms such as her sleeping patterns, stomach problems and flashbacks. Jane reports that she is able to sleep now, as the doctor has given her medication. The vivid images she had a few days earlier have also stopped. From this, Mary concludes that Jane is responding well to the counselling process.

However, Jane is still having lingering doubts about herself and her role in the incident, suggesting that she still has some unresolved issues. Any remaining negative self-talk will have to be dealt with before Jane can move onto the stage of mastery.

Mary asks Jane about these thoughts that she is still having.

Jane: *'I still feel like a failure, a victim'*

So once again, Mary revisits the incident briefly to *reframe* the situation to show Jane that these thoughts are not reasonable.

Mary: *'During our last session you told me that your children were in the house with you and that all you could think about was what would happen to them'*

Jane: *'Yes, that is correct'*

Mary: *'Let us look again at how you coped. Remember that the intruder had a gun and was a direct threat to the children.'*

Jane: *'Yes, he did have a gun and could have shot me or threatened the children if he had the time to look around.'*

Mary: *'Your quick thinking to give him the bag before he found the children prevented him from harming them.'*

Jane: *'Yes, I suppose you are right'*

Mary now uses this argument to show Jane that her perception of her actions during the incident was clouded by emotions and in hindsight, and is not reasonable in the light of the circumstances.

Mary: *'So, in reality, you were not a victim, but rather someone who was in control of the situation and actually saved her children from a violent threat'*

Jane: *'I think I can see that now'*

Jane considers what Mary has pointed out to her, and soon comes to understand and accept that the situation could have been far worse had she acted otherwise. She has reached the turning point in her counselling process where she can let go of the idea of being a helpless victim and begin to see herself as a courageous survivor of a very difficult situation.

To give this new insight an extra boost, Mary asks Jane if she feels strong enough to visualise herself in the kitchen with the intruder again, but this time to use the confidence and understanding she has now gained. In other words, to imagine herself in the scene as courageous and making a confident decision to give him the bag and be rid of him. Jane has to try this exercise a number of times over the next half-hour, each time rating on a scale of one to ten how she feels. After a few attempts, Jane reports that she is certainly feeling less fearful and her body more relaxed.

The changes to Jane's voice and her more confident body-language lead Mary to believe that the changes to Jane's self-talk and the visualisation exercises have been successful. She stresses that Jane should always see herself as a victor and not a victim in this unpleasant incident. If she is able to internalise this new self-talk and self-image, she can let go of any feelings of failure.

MASTERY (STAGE FIVE)

Mary now moves onto the final stage of mastery, in which both she and Jane collaborate in order to deal with Jane's remaining concerns about her family's personal safely. Jane also admits that she is still apprehensive and irritable and can't really concentrate at work. She also has no real enthusiasm for meeting with her friends and has stopped her usual activities.

Mary believes that although Jane is coping well, she is still in the *recoil phase* and her concerns will have to be dealt with if Jane's life is return to normal. Mary therefore guides Jane into the final stage of the counselling process, that of *mastery*.

Mary believes that the time has come to address these and other more practical issues. It seems that while her sister was staying with her, Jane felt more secure and supported. However, Dorothy has now returned to her own home and Jane has a nagging concern about the security of her home and family. The fact that she no longer feels like going out with her friends, also worries her.

Mary introduces the idea of a plan for mastery, a series of steps that will deal with Jane's concerns and allow her to move forward. Jane agrees to this and Mary agrees to collaborate with her to look at practical solutions to any pressing issues. Some of these necessary action-steps may need some lifestyle changes, but as Mary explains the need to her, Jane understands that this plan is important to return her life to normal. It will also give her a sense of purpose and direction.

The plan will have to consider Jane's present home, financial and work circumstances.

When questioning her further, Mary discovers that Jane does not have security gates at home, nor does she have a panic button or access to armed response from a security company. As a single mom she is simply unable to afford these options on her own. Mary continues to engage Jane on this matter and looks at ways she dealt with security in the past as well as before the incident.

Mary: *'How did you get help in the past if you needed it?'*

Jane: *'I used to phone my brother if I needed anything'*

Mary: *'It is clear that to feel more secure you will have to improve your systems at home. 'Is it possible that your brother will help you with security upgrades?'*

Jane mentions that her brother has already offered to have security gates fitted for her. She has also found out that there is a neighbourhood watch operating in the area.

Mary: *'Is joining the neighbourhood watch possible for you?'*

Jane: *'Yes, I suppose that would not be a difficult thing to do'.*

Mary continues to help Jane work through all her concerns, looking at all practical solutions using Jane's past, present and future possible options.

The aim of this session has become to help her with a structured plan of action-steps to cope with her remaining fears, doubts and concerns, and to help her readjust back to her normal lifestyle. This usually takes place during the final phase of the trauma process, that of *re-organisation* and *re-integration.*

As mentioned, these options (action-steps) should be practical, realistic and achievable, and Jane needs to take full responsibility for their implementation in her plan for mastery. For this reason Mary knows that they cannot simply be a set of ideas imposed by her, the counsellor, but rather the outcome of a collaborative planning process.

During the discussion with Mary, Jane agrees that there are a number of simple steps that she can take to improve her personal security. She needs a security gate at the kitchen door, which she uses most of the time to get into her home, and will accept her brother's kind offer. She has also decided to have a panic-button system installed, linked to a local security company, which she can presently get on special offer at an affordable price. She also plans to join the local neighbourhood watch.

Fortunately, Jane's legal issues from the incident have been dealt with. She has claimed from the insurance company for the money she lost and has given her statement to the police, during which time she was helped and supported by her brother.

Regarding her social life, Jane blames her negative moods for not socialising with her old friends. Mary points out that isolating herself socially is not a good idea, as she now needs the love and support of her friends. Mary agrees and they discuss ways in which she can reconnect with her circle of friends. Jane also agrees to see a psychologist if these moods persist. Mary also offers other suggestions to help improve Jane's moods, such as exercise, sports, recreational activities, hobbies and listening to music, as well as following a more healthy diet. Jane decides that she will join the local walking club, as gym membership is too costly. Mary also recommends that Jane consider a new process to lessen her body tension called tapping. This is done by an acupressure specialist who will tap or press on acupressure points to relive body tension. Jane says that she will keep this is mind.

According to her plan Jane will continue visiting her brother and phone her other family members, especially her sister Dorothy, at least once a week. She will try to take the children to her family for weekends and has also decided to contact her church and link up once again with the women's cell group. She also commits to continuing with her daily social media contacts.

As Jane has responded well to the counselling process, Mary believes that medication will not be necessary. Jane appears to be coping with daily challenges and life skills coaching is not needed.

Mary wraps up session three by praising Jane for the progress she has made, as well as having the courage to complete her plan for mastery. Jane is more confident and eager to implement the ideas that she has included in the plan. Mary leaves the counselling room with Jane and arranges for the fourth and possibly final session in two weeks time.

SESSION FOUR

Jane returns to the centre after two weeks for her fourth session of trauma counselling. Her body- language speaks of confidence and she appears visibly more relaxed. She is once again met and greeted by Mary at the door and escorted to her place on the couch.

This is a short session which looks at feedback on Jane's action-plan, as well as any new issues or obstacles to her plan that have arisen in the meantime. At this point, her earlier feelings of fear, helplessness and loss of control, as well as her negative self-talk appear to have been properly managed. Mary therefore concludes that Jane has entered the final phase of the trauma process, that of *reorganisation* and *reintegration*.

Jane informs Mary of the action-steps that she has implemented and that her life is almost back to normal. They spend some time reviewing these steps and Jane's successes. Most unpleasant symptoms have disappeared and she has re-established contact with her friends and family. She has also been able to get more time off work to relax and enjoy herself and feels safer now that her brother has fitted a self-locking security gate at the back door. She does, however, mention that there are still times when she is nervous, such as during the early evening when the incident occurred. She is also apprehensive when she sees men in the street resembling the intruder. Mary once again reassures her that this is normal and that it be a while before she is fully able get over the incident and it becomes only a memory.

Mary suggests that Jane do the relaxation exercise or meditation each time the troubling thoughts or images enter her mind. Jane agrees, as the exercises Mary gave her have been working quite well.

As a final check, Mary once again asks Jane if she has had any flashbacks or negative emotions and thoughts. Jane replies that, apart from the occasional uneasy feelings she mentioned, she is feeling much better. Mary can also see this in her relaxed body language.

Mary agrees that Jane is definitely stronger and more in control than before and tells her that it will not be necessary for her to come in for another face-to-face appointment. She informs Jane that she will phone her in about a month as a follow-up. Jane is very grateful to Mary and they hug and bid each other farewell.

SESSION FIVE (FINAL FOLLOW-UP SESSION)

About a month later Mary phones Jane and they have a short conversation. Jane admits that the original incident was a nightmare, but the fact that she made it through the process has given her a better understanding of herself and her strengths and she feels generally more competent. Minor day-to-day challenges no longer bother her too much, as she knows that she has the resilience and inner strength to face and overcome them. Mary compliments Jane on these new self-insights and points out that self-empowerment is the most important and essential element of mastery. Mary assures Jane that she will be there if Jane ever feels the need to contact her again and ends the call.

CHAPTER FOUR

COUNSELLING LARGE GROUPS OF PEOPLE

It can happen that you are called to the scene of an accident or another incident in which many people are injured or traumatised. For example, the scene of an aircraft disaster at an airport, and you have counsel both survivors as well as family members. Fortunately in such high profile cases there are usually other volunteer counsellors available and you will most likely form part of a team.

CASE STUDY: A BANK ROBBERY

I will not use a worst case scenario for this case study, rather a situation which is more common, such as a bank robbery. In this case study a team of trauma counsellors from a local volunteer counselling centre have been asked to come to the scene to counsel the traumatised bank staff. The robbery has taken place less than an hour ago and there are quite a few bank employees to be attended to.

Each counsellor is given six employees and they have been asked to begin immediately with trauma counselling without first having a debriefing session. This is usually the case when there are many counsellors, and certainly more effective than a debriefing managed by only one person.

A floor manager coordinates the counselling and liaises with the team of counsellors. The bank has closed as a result of the incident and fortunately each counsellor is given a separate private room for counselling. The employees are divided into five groups of six and sent in one at a time by the manager. As soon as the counsellor finishes session one with the first employee, he repeats the process with the remaining five as well. Session one is the most intensive and should take at least an hour per employee. In other words, six employees will take an entire day, allowing for lunch and other breaks. In between clients the counsellor makes brief notes on each case for the follow-up session (session two) the next day. This is important, as some of the employees may be off sick, or the order in which they are sent for counselling may change for other reasons.

SESSION ONE

John is a trained trauma counsellor and has quickly set up the room to be suitable for counselling. As the first employee is brought to him, John introduces himself at the door (first name only), and tells the employee, a woman, that he is a trauma counsellor appointed by the bank to help her. He asks her name and she says it is Sheila. She is in tears. Her body-language shows that she is very distressed and seems quite helpless. John thanks the worker who brought her in, takes her arm and guides her to a chair which he has put close enough to his own to be able to support her.

INTRODUCTION: STAGE ONE

This is stage one as shown in chapter one of this guide. John's aim here is to build a relationship with Sheila and attend to her most damaging emotions and thoughts. His aim is to try to get her to let go of as much of her tension as possible.

He leans forward to show his concern and support for Sheila. His voice is gentle and modulated, suggesting empathy and unconditional positive regard. He continues by reassuring Sheila that he will be with her for the whole process, that the counselling is totally confidential and that any information she shares with him will not be given to management.

Following these reassurances, John does not as yet begin with in-depth counselling, but he first gently responds (attends) to her obvious distress using reflection (in this case, *immediacy*), to help her relax and to build a relationship of trust.

John: *'Sheila, I can see that you are very upset' 'This must be very difficult for you'*

Sheila: *'Yes, this has affected me badly',* she sobs.

John then asks Sheila if she is experiencing any symptoms. She replies that she has a headache, nausea and diarrhoea and her mind is still full of images and negative thoughts of the incident. John reassures her, explaining that this is perfectly normal under the circumstances.

He then briefly outlines the process that he will follow, in which she will be asked to first give him a quick, shortened version of the facts and a bit later, the emotions, feelings or thoughts she had at the time. This will help Sheila get used to the idea of sharing information about the painful incident and prepare her for the deep exploration of emotions and thoughts to come. He is careful to point out that she will not be asked to relive the experience, but to rather to share it with him as a 'story' of the incident. This is to allow her to keep an emotional distance from the actual event.

John tells Sheila that he may interrupt her to clarify certain issues or to identify specific feelings and thoughts. Finally, he asks her permission to continue with this process, explaining that it is the most useful way of assisting her. Knowing what to expect and giving permission allows Sheila a sense of control over the counselling and should help to lessen her feelings of helplessness.

Sheila begins by telling John very briefly how she was involved in the robbery. She is a teller and was directly threatened by the robbers As Sheila continues, John only listens and reflects, making mental notes of the facts. During the robbery one of them came to her window and demanded that she put all the cash in her drawer in a bag. He was swearing at her and very aggressive. She also remembers seeing another robber hitting the manager over the head with a gun.

John has not yet even started to explore emotions, but notices from changes in her body-language that Sheila is showing signs of distress; and she starts crying. He leans forward and puts a hand on her shoulder and use comforting words and a gentle tone of voice to empathise with her.

John: *'I understand that this is difficult for you.'*

Sheila: *'Yes, it is very traumatic'.*

EXPLORING FEELINGS AND THOUGHTS: STAGE TWO AND THREE

John gives Sheila some time to compose herself. He feels at this time that they have established a rapport and built up a relationship, and even though she is distressed, she is not in any danger of being re-traumatised. He therefore moves onto stage two, beginning with the in-depth exploring of her emotions.

He now asks her to go over the incident again step-by-step, but this time he encourages her to get in touch with her feelings and share them freely. However, in order to stop re-traumatisation, he once again tells her she must not try to relive the experience, but rather to view what happened as if she was looking at it from a distance, passing her by on a screen or through a window. In other words, to take on the role of an observer rather than being directly involved.

Even with this strategy in place, Sheila's emotions arise strongly as John listens and reflects, and she breaks down occasionally and needs support. Her emotions of fear, helplessness and loss of control are simply too intense and she is shaking uncontrollably. John is empathetic and assures her that releasing her emotions in this way is positive and necessary for her healing.

John continues to prompt Sheila to share memories of the incident. He pauses to reflect, clarify and question her on each painful feeling or intense emotion that is causing her distress. Although he is focussing on her feelings in this stage, they come out all jumbled up with frightful images and negative thoughts which he also acknowledges and explores further. For their relationship of trust to continue it is important that he acknowledges everything that she says. This takes them into stage three, exploring her thoughts, which now combines with stage two (exploring her emotions).

During his questioning John uncovers that Sheila's most intense feelings arose at specific times when she felt most threatened, for instance, the time when the robber pointed his gun at her and told her to open the drawer with the money.

John: *'What did you feel at that moment?'*

Sheila: *'I felt total fear and helplessness'*

John: *'And what went through your mind?'*

Sheila: *'I thought he was going to shoot me and I was going to die'*

John recognises this vivid image of the pointing gun as Sheila's 'moment of trauma', which led directly to the thoughts that she was 'going to be shot' and 'going to die'. This set off her trauma.

He asks Sheila to finish her account of the incident. At this stage his approach is that of listening, reflecting and exploring her feelings and thoughts as they emerge and he has not posed too many direct questions on her actions during the incident. However, Sheila mentions a moment when she thought of pushing the alarm button under her desk, but was too afraid. John identifies this as an issue of concern that will have to be looked at later.

After about an hour Sheila is reasonably relaxed. John feels that they have made enough progress and wraps up the first session by pointing out to Sheila some of the typical symptoms that she may have during the night and in the next few days. For instance, she may be not sleep properly or have bad dreams and wake up fearful, tense, irritable and nervous. Her medical problems will also continue and may even get worse. Once again he tells her that this is perfectly normal under the circumstances.

John also asks Sheila to try to eat only healthy meals over the next few days and not to drink too much alcohol or take strong medication, as this will only dull her responses and make her recovery more difficult. A glass of wine or headache tablets will be fine.

This information prepares her for the possible problems that she may have and gives her at least a 'heads-up' and some insight into her feelings while she adjusts to the trauma. He also asks Sheila if she has anyone who can stay with her for a few days to help her with the house chores and give her emotional support. Sheila says that she has phoned her friend Joan who will be staying with her for a short while, but Joan is working and will only be there in the evenings.

John tells her that this is fine, as she must, in any event, come to the bank the next morning for the second session of trauma counselling, when he will once again be her counsellor. This comforts Sheila as she has a good relationship with John and now knows that she has ongoing support.

Sheila agrees, and John tells her that he will meet her outside the bank early the next morning when he will continue the counselling process. Sheila hugs John at the door as she leaves. This is a good sign which tells John that she now trusts him.

Once Sheila has finished with John, the manager sends in the second person to be counselled in the same way (Session one). This continues until all six employees have been counselled for the first time. As the process for each client is the same, only this one case study (John and Sheila) will be unpacked in detail.

NOTES:

Research has shown that traumatised persons cope better if they not sitting alone at home but rather back at work with a lighter work-load. At home they may have little or no emotional support, and being busy also helps them to stay focussed and lessens their negative thinking. Employers and co-workers are also usually quite supportive.

Also note that if clients are still in major distress after the first session, it is best to refer them to a psychologist or psychiatrist for medical treatment, or even a hospital if they are out-of-control and need sedation. In this case you would follow up to make sure they are getting treatment or meet up with them at the hospital for later counselling.

SESSION TWO

During this session (session two), John will continue to explore Sheila's emotions as well as those negative thoughts still causing her distress. This is stages two and three of the trauma counselling process. In this session John will also try to begin the empowerment stage (stage four). This may not be the case with the other five employees. It all depends on how well they each responded to session one.

John meets Sheila (and the other five employees) at the door of the bank the next morning as he promised. He escorts Sheila as his first client to the office he is using for the counselling.

Sheila has followed John's advice and reported for work even though she is still feeling very upset. John asks her about her work situation and she tells him that she has been taken away from the front service department and is doing light administrative duties in an office. She is happy with this arrangement.

John begins the second session by asking Sheila about any symptoms she had during the night and any feelings and thoughts which have been particularly bad over the last twenty-four hours. From Sheila's responses, he once again identifies her fear, but this time, also some self-blame. He is careful once again to make sure that she is at an emotional distance from the incident.

NOTE:

Traumatised persons feel fearful and helpless and even blame themselves for what they believe to be wrong actions on their part, or simply having done nothing to prevent or to stop the incident. These feelings are supported by a number of perceptions, thoughts and beliefs which are mostly not accurate and have to be stopped as soon as possible.

These negative thoughts and beliefs do not take into account the complexities and reality of the incident. In other words, it is extremely difficult for a traumatised person to have an objective view of their own actions and this often leads to self-judgement and distress.

John encourages Sheila to allow herself to feel and release these emotions, which she does in the way of sobbing. He shifts closer to her and holds her arm again. In spite of the sobbing, Sheila is definitely in a 'better place' than the previous morning. She once again composes herself.

John now turns his focus to the thoughts and self-incriminating beliefs which he believes are giving rise to these emotions. John has moved through stages two and three and decides to go to stage four, that of *empowerment.*

EMPOWERMENT: STAGE FOUR

From her present state of mind and body-language, he believes that Sheila is strong enough to handle some challenging questions. However, if her emotions flare up again, he would have to return to the earlier two stages and work with those emotions.

John carefully questions Sheila regarding her thoughts during the different stages of the incident. He identifies self-talk which points to her belief that she should have been more courageous and pushed the alarm button under her desk when the robber approached her. This belief is leading to the feelings of guilt and self-blame.

John: *'During the last session you told me that you felt bad about not setting off the alarm.'*

Sheila: *'Yes, I was thinking that the robbers might have run away if I had set off the alarm'*

John: *'And as a result, you blame yourself for the manager being assaulted?'*

Sheila: *'Yes, it would not have happened if I had only acted'*

John gently challenges this belief by *reframing* the situation, pointing out other (worse) possible outcomes if she had behaved differently. Notice how John only uses the information given to him earlier.

John: *'Earlier you told me that he had his gun pointing at you and you felt very threatened?'*

Sheila: *'Yes, that's right'*

John: *'What could have happened if the robber saw you pushing the alarm and panicked?'*

Sheila: *'I suppose he could have shot me. He was very aggressive'*

John: *'So by not pushing the alarm you actually you may have saved your life?'*

Sheila: *'Yes, I suppose that is true'*

John continues to show Sheila other scenarios in which the robbers may have acted differently to the alarm, for instance, employees being shot or severely injured in their haste had the alarm been activated. The actual facts were that they were very aggressive, very determined and well-armed and it is unlikely that an alarm would have sent them running.

His aim is to show Sheila that her view of the situation and the belief that she acted incorrectly, is unfounded and not rational in view of the actual circumstances of the incident. He introduces her to a different perspective on the incident in which she had, by not pushing the alarm and quickly handing over the money, played a key role in keeping the violence to a minimum. Following this reframing of the situation, Sheila appears visibly relieved.

A more important concern to John is attending to the crippling fear that gripped Sheila during the moment of trauma (the sight of the gun pointing at her). This vivid image of the gun had also set off feelings of helplessness and of having no control which only made the fear worse. These feelings are still with her even though she let go of her pent-up emotions in the first session.

The problem is that the beliefs and thoughts which support them are still there, and these will need to be challenged and countered so that these feelings will lessen naturally over time.

John now looks at Sheila's account of the exchange between her and the robber step-by-step.

John: *'What went through your mind when you saw the gun pointed at you?'*

Sheila: 'I thought I was going to die and was very afraid'

John: *'I understand'. 'You were faced with an aggressive robber who wouldn't hesitate to kill you'.*

'You actually did very well to keep calm'. 'Anyone would have felt afraid when faced with that situation'

Sheila: *'Yes, strangely enough, I acted calm at the time, even though I was afraid'*

John: *'So you think you did well?'*

Sheila: *'No. That is the problem. I see myself as a failure as an employee' 'I simply handed the money over to him'*

John: *'Let's look at it again.' 'He pointed the gun at you, you were afraid, but you did not freeze but calmly opened the drawer and handed him the money.'*

'What were you thinking when you did that?'

Sheila (after thinking a while): *'I suppose I thought that by giving him the money I would get them out of the bank quickly so that no one gets hurt.'*

John: *'In other words, it's not true that you were a failure and had no control over the situation. In fact, you were thinking consciously and had a plan to resolve the matter and prevent others from being hurt'*

Sheila: *'I suppose you are right, I wanted them to leave as soon as possible'*

John has acknowledged Sheila's feeling of fear when the gun was pointed directly at her. He has now also looked at the situation more closely and was able to show her that her belief of being a failure is simply not justified in the light of the very real circumstances. He praises her for her actions, pointing out that many people would panic and freeze under similar conditions. In fact, her actions were reasonable and quite courageous, as, even under such extreme duress, she was still thinking of others.

NOTES:

The realisation and acceptance that a person acted reasonably, rationally and had a plan of action during a traumatic incident is extremely empowering and can counter self-recriminating thoughts and beliefs, allowing them to be replaced with more positive thoughts or self-talk.

In Sheila's mind, the belief that she was a failure can now be changed to:

'I am not a failure'

'I was afraid, but was still able to act rationally'

'I actually did quite well under the circumstances'

'I was not helpless, I was consciously thinking'

'I did not lose control during the incident' 'I had a plan'

If Sheila can internalise these new insights over the next few days, John will have succeeded in *restructuring* her negative thinking and self-beliefs. As she changes her view of herself and her actions during the incident from negative to positive, she should gradually be able to let go of the residual feelings of fear, helplessness and loss of control.

In some cases clients may not be able to identify their self-talk, which is often subliminal, and you have to infer and 'offer' thoughts to them. Obviously you would use your experience and common sense in such cases.

For example: *'You said that you are blaming yourself in some way'*

'You are thinking that there was more that you could have done'.

Once they clarify or acknowledge this self-talk offered to them, you can challenge it as before.

At this point John feels that they have made enough progress during this session. Sheila is visibly more relaxed and her state of mind and mood has improved. He once again points out that any upsetting physical symptoms she has over the next few days are normal and he tells her that he will be back in two days again for session three.

John takes Sheila to the door and she hugs him again. In the case of a male counsellor it is fine if a female client initiates the physical contact. John then makes arrangements with the manager to see Sheila in two days time again.

As before, the manager sends in the other employees for session two, one at a time.

SESSION THREE

John has returned to Sheila's workplace for the third session. She has resumed work as a teller at the front desk. Once again, a private office has been set aside by the manager for the counselling. Sheila is already waiting and stands up to hug John as he comes in the room.

After greeting each other, John and Sheila sit down and after a bit of small talk, he picks up where he left off. However, before he continues with the empowerment process, he asks Sheila how she has been sleeping and coping emotionally and if there are still symptoms.

John: *'How are you feeling at the moment?'*

Sheila: *'I am feeling much better, but am irritable sometimes and then want to be left alone.'*

'I am also a bit anxious and nervous, especially when strangers come into the bank'

John: *'Yes, that is quite normal after what you have been through.'*

It seems to John that Sheila has reached the *turning point* in the counselling, where she has let go of her 'victim' consciousness and thinking and is on the path to the mastery of her situation.

However, John believes that she is still in the *recoil* phase of the trauma process and needs more encouragement and empowerment to move onto the final phase, reintegration and reorganisation.

This help will come in the form of practical steps to address the issues which still concern her and the formulation of a plan which will give her the feeling of once again having control over her life. To discover what these issues are, John uses reflection and careful questioning to explore the reasons for Sheila's feelings of anxiety.

John: *'Are you still concerned about your safety at the bank?'*

Sheila: *'Actually no. The bank has placed guards outside to regulate access and has promised to install bullet-proof glass for the tellers. I feel more secure knowing that.'*

John: *'What is still concerning you at this time?'*

Sheila: *'I keep asking myself if I am really safe at home, as I live alone'*

John quickly establishes that Sheila's concerns relate to issues of personal safety at home and the fact that she has no real family who live close by. She also still seems unwilling to go out with her friends. However, he notes that her self-talk has moved away from thoughts of fear, helplessness and self-blame to a more positive view of herself and her actions during the robbery. This shows that the earlier process of cognitive restructuring in session two was successful. He now only has to deal with those thoughts producing her day-to-day concerns and anxieties.

MASTERY: STAGE FIVE

John praises Sheila for what she has achieved in the previous sessions and asks her if they can now look at practical steps to address these concerns, options that will assist her to cope better, to deal with any negative thoughts that remain and return her life more or less to normal. Working together, they will have to compile these steps into a plan for mastery for which Sheila will have to take ownership. For this John will have to use analysing and logical thinking skills.

NOTE:

Any options they decide to include will need to be within Sheila's abilities and frame of reference. This means taking into consideration her level of education, moral beliefs, real-life home and work situations, financial means and coping mechanisms

By this time John knows her personal circumstances and home situation. She is divorced, has no children and is staying alone in a flat situated close to the bank. She does not have security gates or an alarm, panic button or armed response from a security company. John asks her about this in a non-judgemental way and they agree to look at options to improve her security which are within her means. To do this John must look at her past and present methods of security as well as any ideas for her future security.

John: *'Sheila, what have you done in the past to keep yourself safe at home?*

Sheila: *'I usually depended on the neighbours in the flat next door for help if there was any trouble.'*

John: *'Do you think they will continue to keep an eye on you?'*

Sheila: *'Yes, I have spoken to them and they are more than willing to help'*

Working together with Sheila, John looks at a number of other practical, realistic and affordable ways of improving her personal security. These include a security gate at the front door, a contract with a security company and a panic button in the flat. Sheila believes that these changes will give her greater peace of mind. She also believes that her present money situation will allow her to go ahead with these improvements. .

With regard to her family, John supports steps Sheila has already taken to get back and to stay in contact with her family.

John now turns to her social life. As a result of her state of mind, Sheila has been avoiding all the fun times she used to have with her friends. She agrees that this also has to change. Her friends have been a great support for her in the past. John now helps Sheila explore some ideas for getting her back into her social circle and even finding time for more outside activities, such as joining a nearby gym. He points out that fun, enjoyment and good food are important to recover from trauma.

With regard to her medical problems, he refers her back to her doctor.

John now summarises the action-steps Sheila has decided on in her plan for mastery. She seems quite happy with the plan and has written down a lot of the things that she has to do. She agrees to see him again in two weeks time for a final face-to-face session. John takes her to the door where Sheila hugs him again. Finally, John tells the manager that things are going well and he will be coming back in two weeks time. They agree on a date and time when Sheila will be available.

Once again, John sees the rest of his clients one at a time for session three.

SESSION FOUR

Two weeks have passed and John again visits Sheila at work for session four. She seems more relaxed and is smiling. After they are guided into the office set aside for the counselling, John asks Sheila about her remaining symptoms. She says that her medical issues have settled down nicely and she is feeling much better. John also questions her about any leftover stress, troubling images and negative emotions and thoughts she may be having. Sheila says that these have mostly gone away but admits to still being a little tense at times. She believes that she can manage this. John briefly questions her about possible reasons for the tension, but after a while he is satisfied that it is left over from the trauma and getting less as time passes.

This session also focusses largely on practicalities and John has to apply his analysing skills and logical thinking as they go over the results of her plan for mastery. Sheila has had security gates fitted and is having a panic button system installed with armed response from a security company. As a result she feels more at ease. She is also getting out more again and has reconnected with her friends. Sheila's life has almost returned to normal as she has reached out to her family and friends and is spending more time with them. It seem that she is now firmly in the final stage of reorganisation and reintegration and on the road to recovery.

John is very relieved and commends Sheila on the actions she has taken. He tells her that he will contact her again in a month just to check up on how she is managing. She again hugs John and leaves the room to go back to her work station. John tells the manager that Sheila is doing very well but does not share any further details with him.

As before, John finishes session four with the other employees on the same day as well.

NOTE:

You will find that sessions four and five are usually not as long as sessions one, two and three as the client's distressing emotions and negative self-talk are dealt with fully in these earlier sessions.

It could also happen that some of the employees were not as trau-matised as Sheila was (our case study), as they were possibly not directly involved in the robbery, or are simply more resilient, and it may not be necessary to see all of them again for session four.

SESSION FIVE

As Sheila has responded well to counselling, John does not think it is necessary for him to visit her at work again and he now phones to ask how she is doing and how her plan for mastery is going.

Sheila briefly discusses the steps she has taken to put her plan into action and says that she is doing well. Once again, John praises her for the progress she has made over the past weeks and tells her to contact her HR department at any time if she needs more counselling. Sheila is grateful for John's help and he ends the call.

After the phone call, John completes his written report on Sheila's case for the counselling centre. He also does reports on the other employees he counselled.

NOTES:

Some counselling centres want a report on the counselling process and the progress of the client. This should be just a general outline of the process followed and no intimate details given unless the counsellor is being supervised by a psychologist, in which case a detailed report can be given to the psychologist, who is also bound by the ethics of confidentiality. In a supervised programme the psychologist will want regular updates as from session one and will give guidance and advice when there are problems.

If, after session two, there is no clear improvement in a client's emotional state, in other words, he (or she) is still in severe distress and is not responding to the counselling process, the counsellor must inform the supervising psychologist (or the manager of the company if it is not a supervised programme) and refer this client immediately to a clinical psychologist or psychiatrist.

There could also be other complications such as prior illnesses or earlier psychological problems which prevent your client from recovering. This can also happen when counselling is delayed for weeks or even months. If it is untreated, trauma can end up as P.T.S.D. And if this has already happened, you must refer them to a psychiatrist as soon as possible for medical treatment. For more information on P.T.S.D. (Post-traumatic Stress Disorder) consult part one of this guide (Training for lay counsellors).

CHAPTER FIVE

COUNSELLING MANAGERS AND SENIOR STAFF

This case study is an advanced counselling session involving a senior manager. Due to his position there are extra pressures on him, as well as other dynamics, which make the counselling session slightly different to that of employees, enough for me to show it as a separate case study.

When you start counselling you will see that every person and counselling session is different and you must often just use your gut feeling to know what to do or say next. As long as you know your counselling skills and the basic procedure, you will be fine. Respond to what is in front of you. Sometimes you can skip sections of the process and sometimes you will need to remain longer with others. This case study is a little different and shows you the type of flexibility you will need.

Attention to self-empowerment, growth and development of effectiveness and resilience is needed when you are counselling persons in positions of responsibility who have been traumatised. You will find that there are often unrealistic expectations placed on themselves as well as a lack of a clear understanding of their role boundaries and responsibilities. This can weigh heavily on them, leading to very high levels of guilt and self-blame which complicate their recovery.

In this case study the client, David, is counselled by John, a male counsellor.

SESSION ONE

David is the manager of a large bank which has just been robbed by four heavily armed men. During the incident his staff were subjected to threats and abuse, and he himself was directly threatened and hit on his head with a gun.

Once again, a number of trauma counsellors from the centre have been called in to help and each given six employees to counsel. Amongst the employees given to John is the manager, David. John finds his counselling a little different to the rest of the staff as there are other factors involved such as David's managerial perspective and level of responsibility.

INTRODUCTION: STAGE ONE

David enters the counselling room. He is obviously very shaken. John immediately stands up and goes over to meet him. John introduces himself to David as 'John' and says that he has been asked by the company to help him. They both sit down. John sits diagonally opposite David about one-and-a half meters away. This gives him the opportunity to use his peripheral vision to keep an eye on David's body-language.

John leans forward to show his concern and support for David. He wants to build rapport quickly by identifying with him, so he modulates his voice to be reassuring without being patronising, but still showing respect, empathy and positive regard. He tells David that the sessions are totally confidential. Any information he shares will not be given to upper management. Here John is trying to build a relationship of trust.

EXPLORING FEELINGS AND THOUGHTS: STAGE TWO AND THREE

After these reassurances, John sees that David is still looking down and shaking. He seems to be in shock. This means that he is possibly still in the impact phase.

John responds (attends) to David's obvious stress by using reflection (in this case, *immediacy*), to try and help him relax. He goes straight into stage two without first spending time outlining the process as he feels that David is in shock and not really listening. John hopes that David will open up a little even though he has only spent a few moments with him.

John: *'David, I can see that you are very upset'*

David: *'Yes, this has affected me badly'*

John gives David a few moments to gather himself before he continues

John: *'What is it that you feel?'*

David: *'I don't know, I feel numb and am just shaking so badly'.*

John: *Do you have any other symptoms?*

David: *'Yes, I have a terrible headache.'*

John: *'Yes, this is the stress. This is normal for what you have gone through.'*

Here John is normalising David's feelings and symptoms.

John: *'Apart from the numbness, what are you thinking about?'*

David is quiet at first. He is obviously also confused and is still not really hearing what John is saying. John acknowledges his silence and gives him time to respond. Eventually David replies:

David: *'I thought he was going to shoot me'*

John believes that this one thought, which is clearly dominating his thinking, comes from David's 'moment of trauma'. Seeing the gun and realising that it was pointed at him and that he could be shot, was the moment that this thought and the shock response kicked in. John feels that David, who has just shared his most frightening moment with him, will now be more open to counselling.

John is not yet looking at David's emotions or thoughts, as from his body-language he can see that he is still in distress. He leans towards David and uses a lowered tone of voice to empathise with him.

John: *'I understand that this is difficult for you.'*

David: *'Yes, it was very traumatic' 'I felt totally helpless'*

After a few moments John asks David if he is able to give him a quick, shortened version of the incident, just an outline of the event, without focussing on any feelings and thoughts in particular. He hopes that this will prepare him for the deeper sharing later on.

David looks up and with a subdued voice, tells John that he is the manager of the bank and had just opened up for the day and was making sure all the staff were in place when the robbers came in unexpectedly and went directly for him. They knew he had the keys to the safe in the bank. One pointed a gun at him and said that he would shoot if he did not open the safe. David says that at that moment he became confused. Everything was a blur, but he remembers opening the safe and the robbers pushing his staff around and demanding money from the tellers. When he tried to stop them one robber hit him over the head with a gun. Although it seemed like hours, he believes it could not have taken more than a few minutes for them to get the money out of the safe and from the tellers and leave. He said no-one pushed the alarm, as it happened so fast.

David seems a little more relaxed and John now takes the time to explain to him how he will be dealing with the sessions. He is careful to point out that David will not be asked to relive the experience, but to rather to share it with him as if he was only an observer, reviewing scenes from the past. This is to allow David to keep at an emotional distance from the actual event.

John now asks David to go over the incident again step-by-step, but this time to allow the feelings to come out and then to share them with him. He may stop at any time if he feels overwhelmed.

John: *'I have to ask you some difficult questions about what happened'.'If you feel uncomfortable at any time please stop and let me know'*

John also points out that he may interrupt to clear up some facts or to work with specific feelings and thoughts. Finally, he asks David's permission to go along with this process, as it is, unfortunately, the best way of helping him. Knowing what to expect and that he can stop at any time should give David a sense of control over the situation and hopefully lessen his feelings of helplessness.

David: *'I think I must have arrived at the bank at about 8 o'clock'*

John: *'Ummm'*

David: *'When I got there some of the staff were already there'*

John: *'I see'*

David: *'At that time I didn't see anyone suspicious standing around'*

John: *'I understand'*

John supports these brief comments (reflection) by nodding. This 'paralanguage' does not really do anything except to let David know that John is listening and to prompt him to continue.

John continues to ask David to share his memory of the incident. He pauses to reflect, clarify and question him on each painful feeling or intense emotion that is causing his distress. Although he is focussing on David's feelings in this stage, they come out all jumbled up with frightful images of the gun and the violence on his staff, as well as negative thoughts which John also acknowledges and explores further.

John reflects key words and phrases which help him to identify David's emotions and thoughts. Using his body language, tone of voice and choice of words, John shows empathy for what David is saying. In doing so he acknowledges David's feelings and the seriousness of the situation.

David: *'I admit that I was afraid'*

John: *'Afraid?'*

David: *'Yes, I thought I was going to be shot'*

John: *'You thought you were going to die?'*

David: *'Yes, that was the worst moment for me.'*

John has now confirmed that David's most intense feelings arose when he felt most threatened, the time that the robber pointed his gun at him and told him to open the safe.

As John is reflecting David's thoughts, they have entered stage three of the process, which is now combined with stage two (exploring emotions).

Even with the distancing strategies in place, David's emotions sometimes burst through strongly. John listens and reflects, while David stops to regain his composure. It is clear that his emotions of fear, helplessness and loss of control are very intense and he still shakes from time to time. John assures him that releasing his emotions in this way is positive and necessary for his healing.

To lessen his tension, John tries another technique in which he asks David to give him ongoing feedback on the anxiety (tension) he is feeling in his body, rated on a scale of one to ten.

John: *'David, on a scale of one to ten, how would you rate your anxiety at this moment?'*

David: *'I would say an eight'*

John: *'All right. So we know you can handle an eight, but if you feel it going up to nine or ten please let me know and we will take a break.'*

This exercise serves two purposes. First, it gives David a sense of control over the process, and second, it allows John to keep an eye on David's anxiety and find out what he finds most stressful.

David continues by telling John how the tellers were and also threatened by the robbers, and how helpless he felt. John listens and reflects, making mental notes of the facts. From this, apart from the fear and helplessness, John also notes very high levels of guilt and self-blame, as David believes that he should have done something to stop the robbers assaulting his staff and have alerted the authorities.

By this time John has spent an hour with David but feels that he is not ready to move onto stage four, the empowerment stage, and be challenged on his negative thoughts and perceptions of the event. This is in response to David's body language and obvious tension. His stress level is simply too high and he will not be thinking clearly if John moves too quickly.

John: *'I can see that you are still very upset'*

David: *'I do feel better, but I can't stop the shaking'*

John: *'I understand. What I am going to do now is to send you to a friend of mind who is an acupressure specialist to do some work on your body to lessen the tension. Will that be fine with you?'*

David: *'If it will help'*

John picks up the phone and arranges for David to immediately see Dr. James who is an expert in body biofeedback techniques for a session of 'tapping'. What Dr. James will be doing is to ask David to visualise those scenes that are particularly stressful, and as he shares his fear and anxiety, Dr. James will tap or press continuously on certain acupressure points. David will inform Dr. James when pressure on a particular point has a positive effect on his tension using a rating scale of one to ten. This has been shown to be quite effective in reducing body tension.

SESSION TWO

The counsellor, John, returns to the bank the following morning for his second session with David, the bank manager. David says that the tapping session was very good and he has stopped shaking, but during the night he had very bad dreams which brought back all the feelings of fear and helplessness. Once again John reassures David and explains that this is normal under the circumstances.

For the moment David seems in control of his emotions and quite lucid and John decides to slowly move into stage four, that of empowerment.

STAGE FOUR : EMPOWERMENT

While still keeping track of David's emotional state, John begins to reintroduce some of David's earlier negative thoughts and beliefs about himself and his actions. This creates an opportunity for David to reflect on his own unrealistic expectations about the incident. Negative views of one's actions give rise to powerful emotions which can affect one's thinking, and as a result, David's perceptions of his role in the situation do seem distorted. This can be seen in his negative self-talk.

In this stage John challenges David's self-talk to show him that his feelings of guilt and self-blame are actually unfounded. To do this he uses information given to him earlier and offers David new insights into his actions to show that he was not as helpless as he believed, and that he acted with reason, deliberation and intent. If David can accept these new insights, he should be able to finally let go of the crippling emotions and feelings of helplessness, loss of control, guilt and self-blame that are filling his mind.

John uses reflection and direct questioning to call up David's negative self-talk. When he isolates specific strands he sees that David's thinking is becoming more and more negative with each line.

John: *'David, you told me earlier that you felt powerless because you, as the manager, did nothing to prevent the situation in which your staff were assaulted and traumatised'*

David: *'That is what I believe, yes.'*

John: *'And how does that make you feel?'*

David: *'That I am a failure as a manager'*

John: *'And what will be the result of this?'*

David: *'No-one will respect me'*

As you can see, what is in David's mind is a perception that he did nothing based on the common myth that a person must be fully competent (and perfect) in their role and everything they do. This was set off by the belief that he '*should have*' done more, and a lack of belief in himself which he now accepts as reality. He has generalised this judgement to reflect negatively on all his abilities, including his integrity and competence. This has led to negative feelings of helplessness, self-blame, a sense of failure, a fear of rejection and ultimately, a *loss of self-worth.*

John now uses cognitive restructuring to argue against, and try to break these chains of negative self-talk using the true facts of the situation from the information David gave him during the earlier stages of the counselling process. The idea is to challenge and refute these self-beliefs using the power of hindsight, good reasoning and the actual circumstances of the event. Some self-beliefs are simply not true at all when you view them impartially.

John: *'But David, you did do something. When one of your employees was threatened you stopped the robber and were hit over the head with a gun'*

David: *'I can't help thinking that there was more that I could have done'*

John now *reframes* the confrontation to show that, in hindsight, the situation could have been far worse if David had continued to fight with the robbers. In this way John will help David see that his actions were normal, reasonable, considered and indeed correct under the circumstances. In fact, any other action might have had a far worse outcome.

John: *'David, you said they were very aggressive. What do you think could have happened if you had continued to grapple with them?'*

David: *'I think if they thought I was going for the gun they would have shot me.'*

John: *'And if this fighting had caused the other robbers to panic as well?*

David: *'The others had guns as well. I suppose they could have shot other employees in the process'*

John: *'You made your point by interceding for your employee. In the light of what you have just said, do you think that escalating the violence would have been a good idea?'*

(Notice how John points out the implications of any further action by David in terms of 'escalating the violence')

David: *'But I didn't even push the alarm button.'*

John: *'What could have happened if you had pushed the alarm button in front of them?'*

David: *'I suppose they could have panicked and shot me'*

John: *'And possibly some of the tellers as well?'*

David: *'I suppose so'*

John: *'So by not pushing the alarm button you actually stopped the violence?'*

David: *'Yes, I suppose so. They left quickly when they had the money'*

Every situation and set of circumstances is different. In this case John has shown David that his action in not pushing the alarm button while the robbers were watching him was the right one, and that he has nothing to feel guilty about.

However, John sees that David is still agitated and realises that there are still a number of issues that are affecting him. He needs to probe deeper into David's state of mind as the bank manager.

John: *'David, what are your expectations of yourself as a manager?'*

David: *'A manager is responsible for his staff and they have to look up to him as a role model'*

John: *'Do you consider yourself a good manager?'*

David: *'Sometimes I am a good manager, but at times I do doubt myself and my abilities'*

This suggests that David has doubts about himself as a manager and does not clearly understand the role boundaries between being a manager and a *rescuer*. John believes that this could be due to latent insecurities or even personality issues.

John changes his line of questioning to ask about David's background and his job as the manager. He finds out that David comes from a single-parent family and has only recently been promoted to manager. John believes that this means that David has a strong drive to prove himself and his expectations and inflated sense of responsibility have affected his response to the robbery.

John examines this aspect further.

John: *'Do you think it is reasonable to take the blame for all that happened?'*

'Earlier you told me that you had done everything possible to prevent a robbery, such as having security guards and a panic alarm system.'

David: *'Yes but none of that worked during the robbery. There were too many robbers'*

John: *'Yes, the circumstances did not allow for that' 'It was out of your control'*

David: *'I suppose it was out of my control'*

John now boosts David's feelings of competence by showing him that he was thinking rationally and actually had a plan and had some control over the situation.

John: *'Earlier you told me that you gave them the money quickly so that no-one would get hurt?'*

David: *'Yes, I thought that I must get them out of the bank as quickly as possible'*

John: *'That is important, so you actually had a plan to get them out of the bank to stop them from hurting your staff?'*

David: *'Yes, that's true.'*

John: *'From what you said, you were thinking clearly at the time. You had a plan to get them out of the bank as quickly as possible' You were thinking of your staff and in fact, you were not helpless at all.'*

David: *'I suppose that is true.'*

David seems much more relaxed after this in-depth positive exposé of his actions, but John continues to probe even deeper. He now focuses on David's apparent loss of self-respect.

John: *'Earlier you said you believed that no-one would respect you after this'*

David: *'Yes, I did think that at the time'*

John: *'David, but is it true? Do you actually think that your employees think less of you now?'*

David: *'Well, in fact, a number have thanked me for stepping in when they were being threatened by the robbers, so I suppose, no.'*

John now summarises all the facts with a view to showing that David's actions during the robbery were quite reasonable and indeed, commendable. His aim here is to enhance David's feelings of competence and confidence.

John: *'If you look at the whole scenario, you have actually done very well. No-one else was hurt and your staff have actually thanked you for helping them during the incident.'*

This session has taken quite a while and John feels that the last stage of mastery is best left to the next session, as David needs time to think about what he has learnt about himself in this session and let these positive self-insights become his new self-talk. John sees that David's body-posture has improved but he is still a bit apprehensive. He informs David that at the next session they will be working on a plan to improve his relationships with his staff and deal with outstanding security issues at the bank. David seems happy with this arrangement and they agree on another session in about a week's time.

SESSION FOUR

John has come back to the bank after a week for his fourth session
with the manager, David. After a few minutes of small talk, John
believes that David has been successful in internalising more positive
self-truths about himself and his actions during the robbery and is on
the road to recovery.

MASTERY: STAGE FIVE

John now introduces David to stage five of the trauma counselling
process, that of returning a sense of mastery to one's life. He also
points out the importance of steps to address David's outstanding
concerns about the bank's security as well his own work situation.

John stresses the need for David to fully rebuild his confidence as
a manager and to actually be able to enhance his feelings of competence and self-esteem. Although David seems to be coping well,
John believes that David's coping capacity and resilience needs to
be improved. However, he must handle this carefully, so as not to
reflect on David's competency as a manager.

He suggests that David compile a plan for his return to mastery
which will include additional skills to increase his resilience to
stress as well as his effectiveness as a manager. They begin to
discuss options or programs which may help David, such as conflict skills and further management training available through the
company. David agrees to discuss this with his HR department.
They also discuss possible steps to increase security at the bank,
such as bullet-proof glass for the tellers, security cameras and
stricter access control.

David needs to 'own' this plan and it is left up to him to decide on
the content of the plan. Working closely with John, he eventually
decides on a number of realistic and practical action-steps to both
improve security as well as his own skills as a manager. David
agrees to meet with John again in fourteen days time to discuss his
progress with the plan.

In the meantime, John decides to leave David with a parting gift of
a simple skill that he can use to internalise the positive insights he

has gained during the process of counselling. This is how to use *affirmations*. He explains that by repeating a positive self-statement to himself over and over for a number of times each day, such as 'I am a good manager and can cope with any situation', the words will eventually enter his subconscious mind and serve to work against any negativity that is still there. This will also help to improve his feelings of competence. David is grateful for this and they make arrangements for the fifth and final session in two weeks time.

SESSION FIVE

John has returned to the bank for the fifth session of trauma counselling with the manager, David. This final session will deal specifically with the implementation stage of David's plan. David seems much better but still complains of occasionally being tense, especially when groups of strangers enter the bank. John reassures him that this is normal, as it will take a while for him to recover fully from the memory of the event.

John asks how David's plan is getting along and what he has done in the last two weeks. David says that he has been using affirmations daily and his self-talk is definitely more positive. His work is almost back to normal and he is enjoying the material on conflict skills and management given to him by his HR department. They have also arranged for him to see a life coach once a week. The bank has installed closed-circuit TV which is monitored by the consultants at the back of the bank and the bullet-proof glass has been fitted. The staff as a whole now feel a lot safer.

David remarks how his relationship with his staff has actually improved since the incident, as he has been helping them through their own processes of trauma recovery and they appear to have more trust and confidence in him. In other words, his coping capacity and resilience has increased to the point where he is able to help others. He now recognises his strengths and abilities and is able to more clearly define his role as a manager.

The counsellor praises David for his willingness to work with him and the work that he has done in implementing the steps of his action-plan. This has led to him successfully entering the final phase of the trauma process, that of *reorganisation* and *reintegration*. In this case, the reintegration took place within himself as a result of self-discovery and self-empowerment.

NOTE:

This same in-depth probing approach could be used in other cases in which you think that there may be personality or other personal issues hampering your client's recovery. Like an infected wound, sometimes the poison has to be brought to the surface and removed. However, please remember that, as counsellors, you are not allowed to work with actual mental disorders and if you think there are such deep seated problems it is best to refer your client to a professional.

CONCLUSION

An effective trauma counsellor develops a counselling style that is flexible and can be adapted to clients in a variety of situations and with different personalities and needs. These case studies have merely highlighted the key areas and processes needed for trauma counselling, and this guide should be read together with part one 'Trauma Counselling: A practical guide to dealing with Trauma'

MY REFERENCE SOURCES

Barlow, D.H.& Durand, V.M. (2002). *Abnormal psychology: An integrated approach.* (3rd ed.). Belmont : Wadsworth/ Thompson Learning.

Dass, Priscilla (psychologist) (2002), Trauma talk delivered to Lifeline counsellors on 2002-08-06.

Friedman, Merle. (Dr.) (2004). Psych-Action, Trauma Counsellor's Training Course.

Thompson, R. (1996). *Counselling Techniques: Improving Relationships with Others, Ourselves, Our Families, and Our Environment.* USA: Taylor and Francis.

www.health24.com/Mental-Health/Disorders/Tremor-vs-trauma-20120721

www.psychologytoday.com/us/blog/resolution-not-conflict/201110/energy-therapy-acupoint-tapping-the-best-ptsd-treatment

https://www.hgi.org.uk/resources/delve-our-extensive-library/anxiety-ptsd-and-trauma/ptsd-why-some-techniques-treating-it

ABOUT THE AUTHOR

Jimmy Henderson, father, author, Trauma Counsellor-in-Chief

For most of my early career I was a proud member of the South African Police Services. Rising through the ranks and eventually retiring after 30 years of service with the rank of Senior Superintendent. After leaving the police services, I was drawn to continue my calling to help people, counselling in various roles over the next several years.

- Working with Rotary against Crime in establishing trauma centres at police stations, for which I received the Rotary International Community Service Award

- Volunteer work as a Lifeline crisis counsellor and trainer for more than 30 years

- Lecturing in counselling skills at a management college in Durban, South Africa

- Working as a trauma counsellor for a large banking group assisting staff traumatised by bank robberies and hijackings

- Hosting various talks and workshops on trauma for government social work departments as well as NGOs

- Tutoring psychology students online for the University of South Africa

Bitten by the writing-bug early on, I am the author of a several best-selling books all available in eBook form, from Amazon. I also enjoy exploring topics of emotional, mental and spiritual wellness on my online blog. My writing has resulted in invitations to speak on numerous occasions on local radio stations and well as international podcasts.

I completed my Ph.D in Psychology at the age of 64 as well as having a post-graduate certificate in trauma counselling from Psych-Action. I am currently registered with the South African Board for People Practices as a Chartered Professional in Learning and Development.

For those of you who are interested in find out about me, my books or to book me for your event, visit my website www.discoveringyourself.co.za

THANK YOU

A big 'thank you' to readers for buying this e-book and supporting self-published authors. I hope you enjoyed it and that it has helped you with your trauma work or the training of new counsellors.

And for those of you who may also wish to self-publish, I recommend www.myebook.online the company that handled my e-book conversion and placed it on Amazon for your benefit.

INVITATION

Let me invite you to have a look at my other ebooks which are also on Amazon, Barnes and Noble and Smashwords. https://www.amazon.com/Mr.-Jimmy-Henderson/e/B004HS9AYS

In Search of the Oracle (Neo-World, 2002) (e-book and print)

Multi-Dimensional Thinking (Kima Global, 2007) (e-book and print)

Multi-Dimensional Perception (Kima Global 2010) (e-book and print)

Effective Listening skills for Counsellors and Care Givers (Osborne-Porter, 2012) (e-book & print)

How to Interpret your Dreams (Neo-World, 2013) (e-book and print)

Improving your Relationships (Neo-World, 2013) (e-book)

A Guide to Effective Parenting (Neo-World, 2013) (e-book)

A Comprehensive Guide to Crisis Counselling (Neo-World, 2013) (e-book and print)

Printed in Great Britain
by Amazon

66620677R00129